BONES

THE OFFICIAL COMPANION

Bones: The Official Companion
ISBN 10: 1 84576 539 7
ISBN 13: 9781845765392

Published by Titan Books,
A division of Titan Publishing Group Ltd
144 Southwark Street
London
SE1 0UP

First edition October 2007
10 9 8 7 6 5 4 3 2 1

Acknowledgements
The author would like to give special thanks to the cast and crew of *Bones*, especially Hart Hanson, Barry Josephson, Stephen Nathan, Kathy Reichs, David Boreanaz, Emily Deschanel, Michaela Conlin, Eric Millegan, TJ Thyne, and Tamara Taylor. With additional thanks to Debbie Olshan, Lauren Whitney, Kate Miller, and Adriana Lemus. And to everyone at Titan Books, especially Cath Trechman, Adam Newell, Jo Boylett, Martin Stiff, Karl Barr and Rob Farmer.

The publishers would also like to thank the cast and crew of *Bones* for all their help with this book. Particular thanks to Kathy Reichs and Hart Hanson for their fantastic foreword and introduction. Many thanks also to Debbie Olshan and Nicole Spiegel at Twentieth Century Fox.

What did you think of this book? We love to hear from our readers. Please email us at **readerfeedback@titanemail.com** or write to us at the above address.
You can also visit us at **www.titanbooks.com**

To receive advance information, news, competitions, and exclusive Titan offers online, please register as a member by clicking the "sign up" button on our website: **www.titanbooks.com**

A CIP catalogue record for this title is available from the British Library.

Printed and bound in the USA.

Coming soon...

Bones:
The Official Companion Season 3

BONES

THE OFFICIAL COMPANION

PAUL RUDITIS

CONTENTS

FOREWORD

BY KATHY REICHS

A journalist once queried, "What questions are you most frequently asked?" Good one. A question about questions. Like a *Bones* episode. Layers inside layers.

The answer is easy. In descending order: how did you create Temperance Brennan? How did Tempe score a TV series? How does the television character differ from that in your books?

Since authors write about what they know, my novels began with a job. My job. I am a forensic anthropologist. Thus, Temperance Brennan's occupation was a given from the start. So were my plot lines. I draw story ideas from what I do.

Déjà Dead is based on my first serial murder investigation. *Death du Jour* derives from work I performed for the Catholic Church, and from the mass murder-suicides that took place within the Solar Temple cult. *Deadly Decisions* stems from the many bones brought to me *grâce à la* Québec Hells Angels. *Fatal Voyage* is based on my disaster recovery work. *Grave Secrets* was inspired by my participation in the exhumation of a Guatemalan mass grave. *Bare Bones* sprang from moose remains I examined for wildlife agents. *Monday Mourning* grew from three skeletons discovered in a pizza parlor basement. *Cross Bones* draws on my visit to Israel, incorporating strangely unreported Masada bones, a burial box supposedly that of Jesus' brother, James, and a recently looted first-century tomb. *Break No Bones* goes back to my archaeological roots and examines the physical evidence of organ theft. *Bones to Ashes* originated with the discovery of a child's skeleton in the Acadian heartland of Maritime Canada.

Okay. Real crime turned into thrillers. But why the leap to the small screen? The fit seemed natural. A strong leading lady. Stories of murder solved with gizmos and science.

How it all came together is a bit hazy to me. In the end, Barry Josephson liked the idea of a character that could be taken from the lab into varying work situations. Hart Hanson liked the idea of contrast, sometimes conflict, between the pragmatic, intuitive mind-set of the cop versus the deductive, analytical approach of the scientist. Johnny Law versus the squints. Thus, *Bones* was born.

From the outset it was important to me that the heroine of the series differ somewhat from that in my books. If the two were identical, how would that impact future novels?

I often give nicknames to the victims I analyze at my lab. I guess I've done that with *Bones*, labeling the two manifestations of my character "TV Tempe" and "Book Tempe".

TV Tempe is at an earlier stage of life than her literary counterpart. Younger, she is less sophisticated, with pop cultural awareness and people skills that still need polish.

Instead of Montreal or the Carolinas, TV Tempe works in Washington, D.C., a setting I find particularly appropriate. As an undergraduate, I attended American University. The first skeleton I held in my hands was at the Smithsonian's Natural History Museum, a template for the show's Jeffersonian Institution.

Perhaps the fourth most frequently posed question concerns my satisfaction with the show.

As development began, my hope was that the series capture the issues of forensic science, while, simultaneously, showing the humanity of the participants, and the occasional humor needed to preserve emotional

balance. I believe each episode does that beautifully. My role as a producer is to keep the science on track. I think I do a reasonably good job.

In my view, Emily's portrayal of Tempe is perfect. She is a woman and a scientist struggling to control passion, maintain objectivity, and be sensitive to human vulnerability. To maintain humor and grace in a difficult and often heartrending occupation. David's interpretation of Seeley Booth as an old style cop relying on instinct and legwork is dead on.

So Tempe reads evidence while Booth reads people. Things aren't always harmonious, but the chemistry between them couldn't be better.

Eric, Michaela, TJ, and Tamara round out the dream team. Every actor, writer, and producer is a pleasure to work with. And the best part? No one complains when I do dumb things on set.

In sum, *Bones* is all I hoped it would be, with each episode underscoring the dedication of detectives and lab scientists working hand in hand in the pursuit of justice – the camaraderie, the teamwork, and, yes, even the romance. Trust me. It happens. Cops and squints aren't exclusively about bugs and bones.

Below from left to right: Hart Hanson, Stephen Nathan, members of the cast with Kathy Reichs and (far right) Barry Josephson.

INTRODUCTION

BY HART HANSON, EXECUTIVE PRODUCER, BONES

Over the first season of a network television series, the writers, actors, directors, and producers push the show around; in the second season, if you're very fortunate, and everything is gelling and there's chemistry between the major players and the stars align and all your ducks are in a row, the show starts pushing back.

I think that's what people mean when they say a television series finds its identity or voice. It takes on its own personae. All of a sudden it exists *outside* of the efforts of the sweat-stained company that produces it. The series asserts itself as a separate entity – and what an entity.

A series has to be selfish, bossy, and bumptious in order to survive. When you consider that out of the hundreds of series pitched, the dozens ordered to script, the proud few that are ordered to pilot, and the shell-shocked survivors which are ordered to series, and then how very, very, VERY few of those make it through the first season, much less a *second*...

It's a tough world for a fledgling television series; some might call it Darwinian. So it makes sense that once one survives infancy, it's like a Spartan or a Klingon or a Beauty Pageant winner: TOUGH.

Bones started pushing back at us well before the end of season one, and by season two the series had become a real schoolyard bully.

If we tried to make it too much of a crime show, *Bones* pantsed us. If we gave short shrift to the procedural forensics elements, it would dangle us by our ankles from an overpass. If we were too serious we got a wedgie, and if our comedy grew too broad, *Bones* dipped us headfirst into a toilet for a swirlie.

All this is good, of course.

Our first hint that *Bones* might have a life of its own was the electricity between Dr. Temperance Brennan (Emily Deschanel) and Special Agent Seeley Booth (David Boreanaz). No matter what we wanted, the scenes between them sizzled. Then, our cast of squints started to catch fire. Dr. Jack Hodgins (TJ Thyne) and Angela Montenegro (Michaela Conlin) started to make eyes at each other behind our backs. Zack Addy (Eric Millegan) changed his hair and his wardrobe and became a fully-fledged Ph.D. And savvy coroner, Dr. Camille Saroyan (Tamara Taylor) was brought on in order to *die* in episode six of season two, but to our utter surprise the series crammed us into a locker until we agreed that she would recover from the poison and join the team permanently.

Our little series was pushing back big time. We have plans for season three, sure, but all we can really do is hope that *Bones* agrees with us.

In the meantime, thank you for your interest in *Bones*. For maximum enjoyment, I suggest you do what we do here: hang on, catch some heinous murderers, laugh and cry with the squints and referee the sexually charged banter between Brennan and Booth. Oh, and if *Bones* asks for your lunch money, take my advice: just give it up.

BREAKING BONES
THE INSPIRATION BEHIND THE SHOW:
AN INTERVIEW WITH FORENSIC ANTHROPOLOGIST AND BESTSELLING AUTHOR KATHY REICHS

Dr. Kathy Reichs is the woman behind Temperance Brennan both onscreen and in print. A member of a rare field-of-forensic-anthropologists, board certified by the American Board of Forensic Anthropology, Reichs works for the office of the Chief Medical Examiner in the state of North Carolina and for the Laboratoire des Sciences Judiciaires et de Médecine Légale for the province of Quebec. She is also Professor of Anthropology at the University of North Carolina at Charlotte. But she has become best known for her series of books about fictional forensic anthropologist Dr. Temperance Brennan. And that success has led to a television series being made that is inspired by her life and her books. It was not exactly the path she initially saw herself pursuing.

"I actually trained to do archeology," Reichs explains. "And I was doing that. I was working with ancient skeletons and then the police started bringing me cases. Today there is a formal process of board certification as with all the other forensic specialties, but back then that wasn't the case. When the police found bones, they didn't really know what to do with them, so they just took them to this bone person, the anthropologist out at the university, and that's how I started getting cases; that's when I made the shift. I just found doing the forensic anthropology more relevant. It wasn't quite as esoteric or academic as archeology: you could actually impact someone's life."

Reichs' reputation in her field grew, along with her experience. In the course of her career, she has testified on the UN Tribunal on Genocide in Rwanda, helped identify bodies found in mass graves in Guatemala (as Brennan is returning from doing in the pilot episode of *Bones*), and worked at Ground Zero in New York after the terrorist attacks on 9/11. Accompanying her field and lab work, she has also published nonfiction books on forensic anthropology. But all that wasn't enough for her.

"I didn't want to do another journal article," she says. "I didn't want to do another textbook that would be read just by my colleagues. I'd made full professor, which meant I was pretty much free to do what I wanted; so, I thought it would be fun to write fiction – to try something different. And I would also be bringing my science to a broader audience."

The first book in her series was released in 1997, and was titled *Déjà Dead*. It followed Dr. Temperance Brennan, the director of forensic anthropology for the Province of Quebec (and a recent transplant from North Carolina), as she worked to solve a case that only she considered to be the work of a serial killer. The book became a *New York Times* bestseller, won the 1997 Ellis Award for Best First Novel and evolved into a series of successful novels following that character.

It was those books, and a documentary that was produced which explained exactly what it is that Dr. Kathy Reichs does for a living, that caught executive producer Barry Josephson's eye and ultimately led to the creation of *Bones*. Rather than just taking Reichs' books and putting them on television, the producers decided to focus on her real life work for their inspiration, whilst adding a sprinkling of her fictional character, Temperance Brennan, into the mix. "She is a forensic anthropologist by day, and that's based on my character in my book," explains Reichs. "But in her off time, she writes novels – and that's based on me." Furthermore, just to add to the complex twisting of fiction and reality, the name of the character in TV Brennan's novels? Dr. Kathy Reichs.

THE LEG BONE'S CONNECTED TO THE...

INTO SEASON ONE

"Would you like to meet with Barry Josephson to talk about a forensic show?" That was the question executives at Fox studios had for series creator/executive producer Hart Hanson, who had an overall development deal with the studio. His answer was simple: "No. I have no interest in doing a forensic show."

"Just go meet with Barry," the executives replied. "He's an interesting guy."

And Hanson, feeling he owed the studio a show since the pilot he'd been developing hadn't worked out, took the meeting. "So I met with Barry and he gave me a two-hour documentary on Kathy Reichs," Hanson reveals. "A lot of people think our show is based on her novels. It's not. It's based on her life. This two-hour documentary about what she could do was fascinating."

What Kathy Reichs "could do" was something that about fifty people in the world are officially board certified to do. Forensic anthropology was not a familiar discipline and Kathy Reichs has certainly played her part in bringing it into the mainstream, with her series of bestselling novels starring a character loosely based on her life and work named Temperance Brennan.

Booth: ...you're not the only forensic anthropologist in town.

Brennan: Yes, I am. The next nearest is in Montreal. "Parlez-vous Français?"

When executive producer Barry Josephson first learned about Kathy Reichs, he immediately read one of her novels and found exactly what he was looking for in an idea to develop for television. "I loved the character," he says. "I felt very strongly that she could be a series character. It was a kind of science that I had not seen on television before. When you think about all the procedurals that are on TV, the *CSI* shows, which I love, *Law & Order*, *NYPD Blue*, and shows like *Hill Street* that I grew up on, I just thought that if I was ever going to venture out there I'd like to do it with something unique. And I found this character so unique, and that's how it started."

As interesting as Temperance Brennan was, Josephson found her real-life counterpart even more engaging, as he watched the documentary on the author that accompanied the book he had been sent. "The lab was a fascinating setting," he says. "The fact that Kathy wanted to go out in the field more often, but she felt strongly about the lab work as well, that conflict was interesting."

Once Hart Hanson had watched the documentary, he too was hooked on the idea of a show about a forensic anthropologist who helped solve crimes based on the examination of a victim's bones. But a television series needs something more than just the basic premise to hang it on. "Step two was 'Am I going to do a pilot that's like *CSI*?'" Hanson remembers asking himself. "No, that's not my thing. The studio said they knew that, and the network said they knew that. They also said, 'Do *your* version.' And that's how *Bones* started. I thought they were lying to me, but they weren't. They let us do the show we wanted to do."

One of the only concerns the studio did have was that they did not want a show that featured dry brittle bones every week. Based on the research and discussions with

both Reichs and Hanson, Josephson was able to put their minds at ease immediately. "One of the really daunting tasks that a forensic anthropologist has to deal with is that frequently the human remains are extremely compromised. This means we have to find a reason for this character to exist, and the reason is that she's almost like a magician. Sometimes she can be wrong, but most of the time she will be right. But her science is great: it enables her to deduce things from these bits and pieces of evidence that she has. And many times those bones are going to be in some sort of bad situation, like the tub or like exhuming a body in any state of deterioration, and so on. We said to the studio, 'It's not going to be a horror show, but sometimes it won't be easy to look at. We will try to render it in the best way that we can.'"

Though Josephson and Hanson had not worked together before, they found immediately that they shared a vision for the character and for the series. "Hart came in and pitched me all the characters. Every character that's in the show, Hart pitched me on day one," Josephson recalls. "And I was blown away by his pitch, his take and the science in the lab. It just kept getting better and better. So, by the time we went into the casting process with the director of the pilot, Greg Yaitanes, I think Hart and I were very confident about who the characters were."

Now they had the characters, it was just a matter of finding the right actors to fit the roles. Hanson describes the process succinctly: "It was hell," he says. "But it always is in a pilot. Looking for Brennan in particular was a nightmare. There were two things that were really hard: one was finding Brennan, because we always knew we needed an actress who could be sexy, smart and funny. At the same time, trying to find a leading man during pilot season in L.A. – it's impossible."

Then came a phone call from Dana Walden, one of the co-presidents of the studio, she asked if the producers would be interested in meeting with David Boreanaz for the role of FBI Agent Seeley Booth. Hanson's response? "I just said, 'I'll take him right now. I don't have to meet with him. I'll take him right now!' I knew David would be very good for us, particularly in light of everyone else we'd seen. And he turned out to be much more than... I'm one of his biggest

fans, I think. And I did not know he could be so charming. To us he's James Garner." Also a fan of Boreanaz, Josephson adds, "He came to it knowing what he wanted Seeley Booth to be. It seemed like a real happy marriage. Then it was a matter of finding the squints..."

Barry Josephson looks back on the inception of the squints: "When we were doing some early research, outside of the information from Kathy, Hart was working with a police detective named Mike Grasso, and Mike was the one who referred to the scientists as squints. So it became a really unique thing for us: the squints. Who are the squints? And how do we define them as scientists? Always with a little bit of a sense of humor about the work."

If the series was going to be about the relationship between Agent Seeley Booth and Dr. Temperance Brennan, it would be the squints who would fill out their world. They would be the ones to provide the background for the science and serve up the lighter moments to

Booth: Cops get stuck, we bring in people like you. You know, squints. You know... who squint at things.

Brennan: Oh, you mean people with very high IQs and basic reasoning skills?

Booth: Yeah.

balance out the darker crimes. Josephson likens the squints to their real-world counterparts: "Kathy talks about going to a pizza place to eat and how other people would move progressively further and further away from their table as they talked about the sort of gross goings-on in their lives. That idea was a big consideration when the actors read for the parts. Do they have the weight? Are they good enough actors to play these characters?

"We were lucky when TJ Thyne came in and read," Josephson continues. "It was easy for me, Greg Yaitanes and Hart to see that this guy could be Hodgins. When Michaela Conlin came in, it was after a long search of many different actors. We felt like she could be Brennan's soul mate; she could also be sassy and she could be a world traveler. It felt like she really fit the part well. And Eric Millegan as the doctoral student just seemed great. Nobody speaks expositional dialogue quicker than Eric. We love him for a lot of reasons, and we love him for that. He's odd, he's offbeat, and I think it really works for that character." Rounding out the cast of supporting players in

Booth: F.B.I., Special Agent Seeley Booth, Major Crime Investigation, D.C. Bones identifies bodies for us.

Brennan: Don't call me Bones. And I do more than identify.

Booth: She also writes books.

the ensemble was Jonathan Adams as the archeologist administrator overseeing them all, and acting as something of a father figure and a voice of reason in this often eccentric world.

However, they were still without the central character for the series. At the time, the working title for the show was *Brennan* and they didn't have their Brennan. Then Barry Josephson spoke with a friend at Disney who had a recommendation. "He told me about Emily Deschanel," Josephson recalls. "He said, 'There's this girl in [the movie] *Glory Road*. She doesn't have a big part but she is fantastic.' I replied, 'I'll try and get a meeting with her right away.' The next day, Hart and I met with her. We pitched her the story and gave her the script. Within three days she was cast as Temperance Brennan."

Hanson also vividly remembers how difficult it was to find their Brennan. They kept seeing great actresses but they only had two of the three important qualities they were looking for. "It was so hard," he explains. "Someone would be smart and funny, but not sexy. Or they were funny and sexy, but not smart. And then Emily came in and read with David and we had that thing. Bang. We just knew right away."

They had their cast. The script was ready. But there was still one piece of the puzzle that didn't quite fit right. "We agonized about a title," reveals Hanson, who at that point was still referring to the show as *Brennan*. "Initially, we thought it was going to be a single person lead, that we would find Temperance Brennan and she would work with a number of different law enforcement agencies. Then we saw Emily and David working together and thought, 'Oh, we've got a much better thing to do here.' 'Bones' is her nickname and it's the start of every story; it's the bones. So we thought, 'Yeah, that's good. That's better than just *Brennan*.' And, this way, it was easier to acknowledge that it was more of an ensemble piece than a single lead character."

So they had a title. The ensemble was in place. They had found their setting in the medico-legal lab at the Jeffersonian Institute in Washington, D.C. The romantic comedy aspect of the show was established by the clear chemistry between the two leads. Now all they needed were the stories...

SEASON ONE

Regular cast:

David Boreanaz: *Special Agent Seeley Booth*

Emily Deschanel: *Dr. Temperance Brennan*

Michaela Conlin: *Angela Montenegro*

Eric Millegan: *Zack Addy*

TJ Thyne: *Dr. Jack Hodgins*

Jonathan Adams: *Dr. Daniel Goodman*

PILOT

WRITTEN BY HART HANSON DIRECTED BY GREG YAITANES

GUEST STARRING: SAM TRAMMELL (KEN THOMPSON), CHRIS CONNER (OLIVER LAURIER), LARRY POINDEXTER (SENATOR BETHLEHEM), TYREES ALLEN (TED ELLER), BONITA FRIEDERICY (SHARON ELLER), DOMINIC FUMUSA (PETER ST. JAMES), DAVE ROBERSON (BENNETT GIBSON)

FBI Agent Seeley Booth meets Dr. Temperance Brennan, a forensic anthropologist and author, at the airport. He asks for her services on a case in which remains were found at Arlington National Cemetery. Brennan is reluctant to help because on their last case Booth failed to give credence to her description of the murderer and murder weapon, simply because it was based solely on an examination of the victim's autopsy X-rays. No matter that she turned out to be correct.

Under pressure from the head of the medico-legal department at the Jeffersonian Anthropology Unit, Dr. Daniel Goodman, Brennan agrees to work the case, contingent on her being granted full participation in the investigation. Brennan brings her team of scientists in on the case, including doctoral student, Zack Addy, "bug and slime guy" Dr. Jack Hodgins, and forensic artist, Angela Montenegro.

Brennan's blunt manner and impetuous actions put Booth's role in the case in jeopardy, but her involvement ultimately leads to the capture of the killer. When she witnesses the murderer destroying evidence at his residence, she shoots him in the leg to stop him.

The volatile relationship between Booth and Brennan is immediately established when he sets Homeland Security on her as she returns from a "vacation" identifying bodies from a mass grave in Guatemala. Through the arguing and banter, there's clearly a mutual respect for one another's work... and maybe something more.

Brennan: I find you very condescending.

Booth: Me? I'm condescending? I'm not the one whose gotta mention that she's got a doctorate every five minutes.

Brennan: I am the one with the doctorate.

Booth: Yeah? Well, you know what? I'm the one with a badge and a gun.

- A decomposing corpse is found in a pond at Arlington National Cemetery, along with small bone remains initially thought to be from a frog. **Epiphysis** fusion indicates the victim's age is between eighteen and twenty-two. Pelvic bone shape shows that the victim was female.
- Silt collected from the pond contains three larval stages of **trichoptera** and **chironomidae**, indicating that the body was in the pond for a year and a half.
- Using tissue markers on the reconstructed skull, an image of the victim is created on the three-dimensional imaging unit (known informally as the Angelator). The victim is identified as Cleo Louise Eller, a missing intern rumored to have been having an affair with a senator.
- Pupal casings reveal the victim was taking medication related to morning sickness, suggesting that the small bone fragments found in the silt were fetal remains.
- The victim was stabbed five to eight times with a military issue k-bar knife. All other damage to the body was done to hide the identity of the victim. Post mortem cranial fragmentation suggests a twenty-pound hammer was used on the victim while her head rested on a cement floor containing traces of diatomaceous earth.
- The diatomaceous earth is linked to a fish tank filter in the home of Ken Thompson, the senator's aide and the victim's boyfriend.

"What's great is that the primary disagreement they have is over relationships, love and romance," says writer/executive producer Stephen Nathan, "which keeps us going forever because it's very sincere. Hart [Hanson] did a brilliant thing when he created the characters, because what is keeping them apart is very organic. The attraction is there and it's undeniable and if they both had a little sodium pentothal in them, they would admit it. But it's very natural and real that they don't acknowledge that, given their personalities."

Both the actors who play the lead roles agree that the relationship between Booth and Brennan is what drew them to the series in the first place. "I think that they're two people who are pretty much made for each other," says Emily Deschanel. "They're both so dedicated to their work. They may have different ways of solving crimes, but they have both dedicated their lives to solving murders. They both have their own issues in their personal lives. They're both stubborn and headstrong. But here are two people who bicker with each other about things because they don't really know how to deal with their feelings for each other."

David Boreanaz concurs, adding, "You can really compare it to *It Happened One Night*. Look at that film for a good formula for what the show is and could be. I think that that's the strength of how these two characters operate and respect each other and how they grow with each other in their lives – and how they deal with stuff outside their lives. For me, that's what the show's all about."

Epiphysis: End of a long bone initially separated by cartilage that fuses with the main bone over time. The growth rate of this fusion can be tracked to determine age.

Trichoptera: Caddisflies. An exclusively aquatic order of insects.

Chironomidae: Midges. Insects commonly found around water.

'Collide' by Howie Day, *Stop the World Now*

'Pain on Pain' by Feeder, *Pushing the Senses*

'Gone' by Thirteen Senses, *The Invitation*

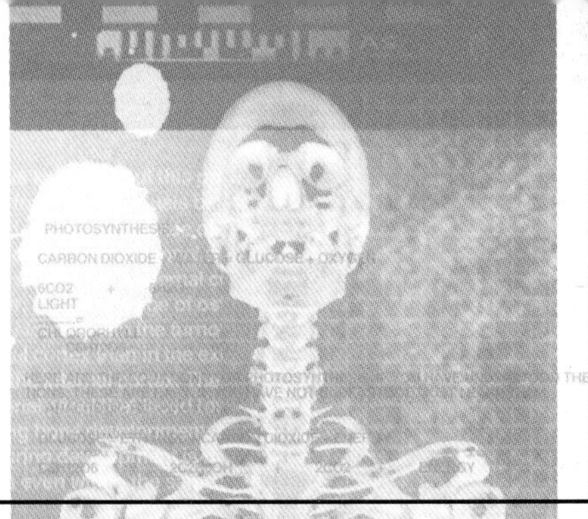

THE MAN IN THE SUV

WRITTEN BY STEPHEN NATHAN *DIRECTED BY* ALLAN KROEKER

GUEST STARRING: JOSÉ ZÚÑIGA (SPECIAL AGENT MICKEY SANTANA), BAHAR SOOMEKH (SAHAR MASRUK), DAVE ROBERSON (BENNETT GIBSON), ANNE DUDEK (TESSA JANKOW), FEDERICO DORDEI (ALI LADJAVARDI)

- An SUV explodes outside a Washington D.C. café, leaving four dead and fifteen injured. The vehicle is registered to Hamrid Masruk, the head of the Arab-American Friendship League and an associate of the President.
- **Dermestes maculatus** are used to clean the charred flesh from the bones, which are then compared to the medical records of Masruk. Examination of the **pubic symphysis**, **cranial vault sutures**, and growth patterns in the vertebrae provide a statistical match.
- While attempting the skull reconstruction, the remains are found to be composed of unusually soft bone tissue. That, combined with the victim's medical records, suggests that he'd been exposed to a toxin.
- The stomach contents of the beetles used to clean the flesh from Masruk's bones are examined to determine the toxin as dioxin. Based on the saturation levels of the toxin, the approximate date of ingestion is revealed to be four months prior to his death.
- As a side project, Hodgins and Zack reconstruct the bomb. They trace the insulation used back to a Woodley Park neighborhood, which is where the victim's brother lives. An examination of the residence reveals the ingredients for another bomb, indicating that the victim's brother was behind the attack and murder.

The charred remains of the driver of an SUV that exploded outside a Washington café are far from the worst Brennan has seen. Angela, however, has trouble stomaching the sight as the investigation begins. The case touches on the sensitive topics of terrorism in America, the profiling of Arab Americans, and governmental interagency cooperation. Booth is warned to tread carefully when a mole from Homeland Security is involved, but that doesn't stop him from putting Bones on the case to get some information out of the agent, since she's not officially an employee of the FBI.

When Brennan brings some files to Booth's home, she learns that he is in a relationship with a corporate lawyer named Tessa. This information proves a nice distraction for Angela from the gruesome case as she sets out to learn all that she can about Booth's relationship.

The case ends with Booth and Brennan stopping a second bombing. Booth is reluctant to shoot the suspect, even though Brennan confirms that visual markers conform with the suspect. It isn't until Brennan calls the man's name and Booth gets a facial confirmation that he is willing to bring his sniper training to bear. He fires, hitting his mark and killing the man before he can activate the bomb.

Booth's history as a former ranger and sniper comes into play throughout the series, but this is the first time we see his exceptional skills really put to use. To get that professional air, David Boreanaz works with police technical advisor Mike Grasso. Often the two go out to the shooting range where they practice with

Booth: I prefer if we would just stay on point and talk about things that you like to talk about. Like dead people. Dead bodies.

Brennan: Sure. Sure. You've killed a lot of people, right? When you were a sniper?

Booth: Maybe we shouldn't talk at all.

targets in scenarios Grasso creates that Boreanaz admits are "pretty challenging".

But just how challenging are the scenarios? No matter how method the acting, there are only so many things an advisor can do to make an actor understand the pressure of being a sniper. According to Grasso, "One of the times that we went out to shoot, I had him sit and wait and hold his breath; and then push his breath out and fire a hundred yards at a little four-inch disk. I told him at the beginning of the day, 'Okay, you're a sniper. And you know how to do this because I've trained you already. Here's the deal: you have to shoot this clay pigeon at a hundred yards. If you miss, we're packing up all our stuff and we're going home. But, if you hit it, we go on.'"

Though it may seem harsh to call off their entire practice for missing one shot, Grasso's point was that a sniper only gets that one shot. "I said to David, 'I can't put you under any other pressure,'" Grasso recalls. "'I can't say that the country needs you or your kids need you. Here's how simple it is: you want to do this today. Well, we're not going to do it if you miss.' And he made the shot. He broke the center of the target out." And their training continued for the day.

Dermestes maculatus: Flesh-eating beetles.
Pubic symphysis: A cartilaginous joint in the pubic bone. The surface of the joint is worn throughout life at a predictable rate that can be used to determine age.
Cranial vault sutures: Fibrous membrane that exists between the bones in the portion of the skull that overlies the brain.

'I Turn My Camera On' by Spoon, *Gimme Fiction*
'Every Ship Must Sail Away' by Blue Merle, *Burning in the Sun*
'Shalom' by Moonraker, *Moonraker*
'Try' by Deep Audio, *Digital Poetry*

A BOY IN A TREE

WRITTEN BY HART HANSON DIRECTED BY PATRICK NORRIS

GUEST STARRING: JOSÉ ZÚÑIGA (SPECIAL AGENT MICKEY SANTANA), HEAVY D (SID SHAPIRO), MARK TOTTY (LEO SANDERS), TOM DUGAN (HEADMASTER RONSON), MARLENE FORTE (AMBASSADOR OLIVOS), CARLOS CERVANTES (ORALDO), MANDY JUNE TURPIN (DAWN ST. JAMES), NICHOLAS HORMANN (LAWYER)

- A body is found suspended from a tree at a prestigious prep school in a small town in Maryland. The deceased is male, approximately five-foot, six-inches tall and 130 pounds. Visual examination of the sternum and skull suggest mid-adolescence, approximately fourteen to seventeen years of age.
- A **cochlear implant** in the ear canal bears a serial number that identifies the victim as Nestor Olivos, a student at the school.
- Time of death is determined to be ten to fourteen days earlier, based on a study of the insects that fed on the body. **Tabanid maggot** pupal casings indicate he ingested a heavy dose of ketamine before he died.
- The victim's **hyoid** bone is broken, which is unusual in a person so young. It is conjectured that the ketamine could have caused the victim to regurgitate while he was choking. The rope held the gastric juices in the upper throat, weakening the hyoid to the point where it broke.
- While searching the boy's room, a DVD is recovered showing the boy engaged in a sexual encounter with a student named Camden Destry. The investigation reveals that Camden and Nestor's roommate were involved in a sexual-blackmailing scheme. The two students killed the victim when he was about to reveal their plan.

Though the case initially looks to be a suicide, Booth's natural distrust for any exclusive school – combined with his gut instinct – makes him more interested in proving it is a murder. Dr. Brennan and Zack, both products of similar educational backgrounds, attempt to provide an alternate perspective, while they focus on developing their working relationship with Booth. Zack especially is in need of more friends when a failed liaison with a female co-worker forces him to seek advice from his colleagues on the art of pleasing women.

While they work on the case, Booth introduces Brennan to Sid Shapiro, the proprietor of Wong Foo's and an expert on choosing the proper meal for his patrons. This comes with the unanticipated bonus of the rest of the team joining them. Though Booth resents the squints stepping on his territory, Brennan rewards him with his own Jeffersonian ID badge.

With a new television series, the writers and actors are working to develop the relationship between the characters onscreen, so the audience understands who they are. But, as with any new job, the same process is happening off-screen as well. "This episode was the first time we had worked with the show's crew," notes makeup effects artist Chris Yagher. "We were just getting to know everyone and had not yet established a working rapport with them."

In addition to setting up the process, the special effects makeup team, lead by Kevin and Chris Yagher, had the added challenge of creating a body that had to do

Zack: Sometime when you're not busy, I wonder if I could ask you a few questions about sexual positions?

Booth: If you even try, I will take out my gun and shoot you between the eyes.

more than just lie on a slab to be autopsied. This one needed to be suspended from a tree and then dropped about twenty feet. "We met with the special effects department a few days before shooting and discussed placing a remote-controlled latch in the head and neck," Yagher explains. "Upon activation, the latch was supposed to disconnect the head from the neck, allowing the head to fall off. As the cameras rolled on the day of shooting, the special effects technician pressed the button – and nothing happened. We tried it again, and again. Nothing happened. Of course, this mishap was not how we wanted to introduce ourselves to the rest of the crew!"

In production, time most certainly is money. With every minute that passes, people start calculating the cost of overtime and just how long they are scheduled to be at the location. All of this, combined with wanting to get off on the right foot when starting a new working relationship, can make a simple technical glitch into a stressful situation. How they dealt with the problem could affect how the crew gelled over the rest of the series. "We stayed calm," Yagher recalls, "and worked with the special effects tech to rig up a cable connected directly with the latch. On cue, the cable was pulled from down below and the head finally fell off. What a relief! After dropping the body into frame on another take, we completed our first day on the show."

Cochlear implant: Hearing aid.

Tabanid maggot: Members of the tabanidae family of bloodsucking flies.

Hyoid: A horseshoe shaped bone found in the human neck.

'Miles from Monterey' by West Indian Girl, *West Indian Girl*

'Sunshine Everywhere' by Deep Audio, *Digital Poetry*

'City Streets' by Positive Flow, *Can You Feel It*

'Cold Hands, Warm Heart' by Brendan Benson, *Alternative to Love*

THE MAN IN THE BEAR

WRITTEN BY LAURA WOLNER DIRECTED BY ALLAN KROEKER

GUEST STARRING: ALEX CARTER (DR. ANDREW RIGBY), MARGUERITE MACINTYRE (DR. DENISE RANDALL), TOM KIESCHE (SHERIFF CHRIS SCUTTER), STEVE REEVIS (RANGER SHERMAN RIVERS), RUSTY JOINER (CHARLIE), KD AUBERT (TONI)

- A human arm is found in the stomach contents of a dead bear in Washington State. **Kerf** marks on the hand indicate that the body-part was severed prior to being fed to the bear, implying the victim was murdered. Booth and Brennan travel to the location to investigate.
- Tests reveal that the arm belonged to a male who died approximately a week earlier.
- Bite marks in a double cusp pattern on the bone suggest that a human chewed on the remains before the bear did, which could make it a case of cannibalism.
- Bear scat contains a piece of skin with a tattoo matching that of a missing student named Adam Langer.
- Remnants of Oregon white truffle with boring dust are also found in the bear scat, signifying that the animal fed on a tree infested with beetles.
- Ranger Rivers tracks the bear's route back to the tree for Booth and Brennan. At the tree they find the remains of Adam Langer, as well as those of another missing hiker, Ann Noyes — who is also missing her heart.
- Indentations on Ann Noyes' bones are determined to be from a sternum spreader that was used to remove her heart, pointing to the murderer being local doctor, Andrew Rigby, who shows signs of **Prion disease**.

Although previously insistent that she be allowed more fieldwork, Dr. Brennan is initially reluctant to make the trip out of the lab to the small town in Washington State. Part of the reason Goodman sends her on the trip is because he thinks connecting with other people would be good for her, since she spends so much time in the lab. Considering the small town they visit is largely populated by single men, Brennan has ample opportunities to connect. Much of her down time on the case is spent with the local men flirting with her, while Booth looks on.

Flirting with strangers is not exclusive to the fieldwork in this case, though. As Brennan continues to ship remains to the Jeffersonian, Hodgins and Zack vie for the attention of the comely courier, who, much to Hodgins' delight and Zack's confusion, is ultimately more interested in Angela.

Location plays a major role in the filming of *Bones*. Though the series is set in Washington, D.C. it is filmed in Los Angeles. And having a federal agent as a character means the series can be opened up to the rest of the United States. The problem is that budget concerns keep the production in town. Thankfully, there are tricks to get around that. According to co-executive producer Steve Beers, "That little town that we found for this episode was actually just the top of a street in Altadena [a suburb of L.A.]. It was two blocks with the [San Gabriel] mountains behind it. But if you look at it a certain way

Booth: You're a smart-ass. You know that?

Brennan: Objectively, I'd say I'm very smart. Although it has nothing to do with my ass.

you could say, 'Yeah, that's a town.'"

As for the forest, L.A. conveniently has wooded areas in the middle of the city. "There's a place called Cedar Grove at the top of Griffith Park," Beers continues. "It's maybe a half acre or an acre. If you stand there and look in certain directions, you see Silverlake and downtown in one direction and Hollywood in another. But there are areas where you're in the middle of the forest and it's gorgeous. You can go up there and work with your production designer and your director and you can actually feel as if you're out in the middle of the woods."

As well as the challenge of finding a convincing wooded location in the middle of L.A. the production also had to produce a convincing bear carcass, another typical challenge for the makeup effects team. "As usual, we had a limited amount of time and knew we could not sculpt, mold and pour up a bear carcass by the time the cameras rolled," explains Chris Yagher. "Instead, we acquired a bear skin from a local taxidermist and built a foam understructure for the skin. Because the bear had to be shown in the middle of a necropsy, we used curing silicone to sculpt the bear's torso muscles directly onto the understructure, and created and attached torso-skin flaps using the same technique. The bear paws were fabricated from foam sheeting, covered in latex, and attached to fake fur we had in stock. Finally, we cut a slit in the torso muscle and dressed the edge of the slit with more curing silicone." And thus the bear was born... and died.

Kerf: The cut or width of a cut made from a tool like an ax or saw.

Prion disease: A mental condition caused by eating human flesh. Symptoms include delusions, erratic behavior, and violent outbursts.

'Looking at the World from the Bottom of a Well' by Mike Doughty, Haughty Melodic

'Big Me' by Peter Himmelman

A BOY IN A BUSH

WRITTEN BY STEVE BLACKMAN & GREG BALL
DIRECTED BY JESÚS SALVADOR TREVIÑO

GUEST STARRING: PAUL BUTCHER (SHAWN COOK), EVAN ELLINGSON (DAVID COOK), NATACHA ROI (MARGARET SANDERS), MICHELLE ANNE JOHNSON (SARA JOHNSON), PAUL PARDUCCI (CAPT. KYLE HENNING), KATHLEEN M. DARCY (ELLIE NELSON)

The team is deeply moved by the death of the missing child. Angela is so affected by the case that she considers leaving the Jeffersonian, noting that it's the longest she's ever held a job. Brennan is particularly upset by the treatment of the victim's foster brothers, as she was a foster child herself after her parents disappeared when she was fifteen. She is able to use that connection to help solve the case — by bonding with the child who felt responsible for his brother's death.

Separate from the case, when Dr. Goodman insists the squints attend a donor banquet, Hodgins is extremely reluctant to go. When Zack reveals to Angela and Booth that Hodgins is wealthy, they figure out that his family owns the Cantilever Group, a powerful company and the Jeffersonian's largest benefactor. Booth pulls Hodgins to work on a case, giving him an excuse to miss the banquet.

Chris Yagher cites the body made by the make-up effects department for the young victim in this episode as among his favorite works created for the show so far because, he says, of the "amount of emotion it stirs up in others." As it's portrayed onscreen, even the characters who have witnessed horrible atrocities are understandably moved by working with a child's remains.

"After working in the makeup effects industry for twenty years, I find it easy to distance myself from what the effects represent and to focus on them just as pieces of artwork," Yagher says. "I see the materials and colors used and the 'brush strokes'. I compare them to what they represent, but this is mainly done from a technical standpoint. I ask myself if the coloring,

Booth: You're actually one of them, aren't you?

Angela: One of who?

Booth: A squint. I mean you look normal and you act normal but you're actually one of them.

- An anonymous call reported human remains in a field outside a local suburban mall. The FBI believes that it could be the body of Charlie Sanders, a child recently reported missing. A **thermal imager** is used to locate the body. Clothing found neatly folded a few yards from the remains suggests a sexual assault.
- Examination of the bones reveals **greenstick fractures** on ribs four, five, six and seven. The sternum is snapped in two places, suggesting the victim was crushed to death by someone of considerable weight pressing down on his chest.
- The scent of chloroform is detected in the victim's mouth. Samples are taken from the mouth, jaw, sinuses, and the remains of the esophagus. The chem lab mass spectrometer identifies the particulates as fluoride at a high level, such as those found in wood preservatives, paint thinners, car wax, or various other industrial products.
- A mass recognition program is modified to scan the surveillance tapes at the mall where the boy was abducted. The tapes show that Charlie's foster brother, Shawn, took him from the mall. Shawn finally admits that he brought Charlie to meet a neighbor, who sexually assaulted the boy and accidentally killed him by pressing down on his chest to keep him quiet.

texture, positioning of the body, tearing of the flesh are similar to the photos I have seen while conducting my research. I also find myself looking at the those photos in a very technical way. That being said, the body of Charlie probably impacted me the most. I have two toddlers, a daughter and a son, and would hate to think that either of them would experience what this character did."

On what initially seems to be a lighter note, the subplot in which the audience learns of Hodgins' wealth actually has deeper undertones for the character: "I think it's a really great quality of Jack's, the way he doesn't flaunt his wealth," notes Hodgins' alter ego TJ Thyne. "He wants people to take him for what he is, not what his enormous net-worth is. It was a big deal to Jack that Brennan should not find out. See, it was Temperance who hired Jack. She hired him for his ability, for his smarts, for who he is as a rubber-to-the-road, hardball scientist, like her. And together they make an amazing team – the stuff that these two can deduce and figure out is pretty mind-boggling. She didn't hire him because of what his last name is or how much money he contributes to the Institute. Jack never wanted her to see him as anything but the best scientist she could possibly work with. I really like that about him."

Thermal imager: A portable device that enables the wearer to see heat residue, such as that released from decomposing bodies.

Greenstick fracture: An incomplete break — common in children due to the pliability of their bones — where one side of the bone is broken while the other side is only bent.

'Some of Us' by Starsailor, *Silence is Easy*

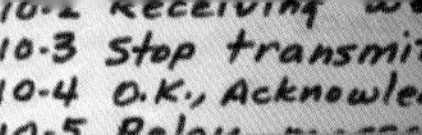

AUTOPSY REPORT

JEFFERSONIAN INSTITUTE

Report No.

Date of Examined.

Subject. *victim Identification*

Staff at the medico-legal unit of the Jeffersonian are often faced with the most difficult cases. Whether a body is brought in for anthropological study or in a criminal case, the remains are often in an advanced stage of decomposition and/or missing key components entirely, making identification of the subject a challenge. The Jeffersonian staff is uniquely trained in the various methods of forensic identification, making even the most complex case manageable.

Bone Markers

Prior to attempting a specific identity match, certain bone markers can indicate much about an individual. The shape of the pelvic bone is most useful in determining the gender of a body. The female pelvic bone is broad and shallow, with a wider pubic arch and birth canal, while the male equivalent is much heavier and narrower.

Epiphysis fusion is the primary indicator in determining the age of a younger victim. The epiphysial plate (often referred to as the growth plate) consists of cartilage found in the long bones of children and adolescents. Over time, this cartilage hardens and solidifies, causing longitudinal growth of the body as a child ages.

Fingerprints and Dental Records

For a specific identification of a body, a forensic scientist relies primarily on fingerprint matching or dental records, if available. Fingerprinting is one of the oldest and most relied on methods for identifying a victim or suspect. However, due to the advanced state of decay or condition of a body, obtaining a complete fingerprint can be difficult. Partial print identification can be used, as well as ways of reconstructing a fingerprint. In one extreme example of a body

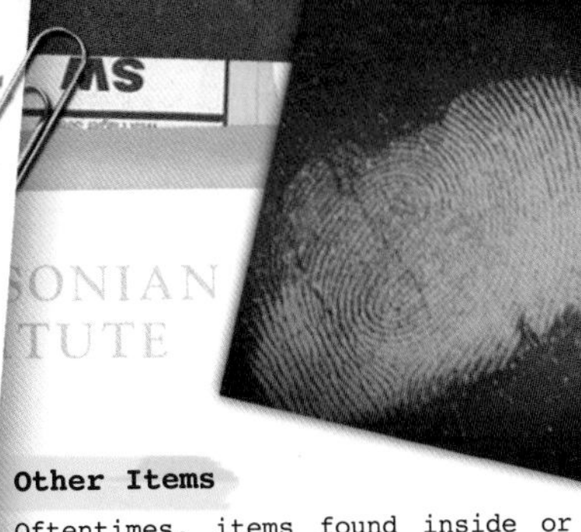

that had become mummified ('The Man in the Wall') the fingers were so dry and parched that no clear fingerprint could be obtained. Dr. Brennan rehydrated the hand, removed it from the victim's skeleton, and then slipped the skin over her own, gloved hand to fill out the fingers so a print could be taken.

Skull Reconstruction

Particularly when in combination with the Jeffersonian's breakthrough technology known as the Angelator (See Research File #2, P44), skull reconstruction is often useful in determining the identification of a victim. Tissue markers placed on the skull, once all flesh is removed, provide an estimate of the skin depth. Environmental factors and evidence found on the subject's body can help estimate coloring of the skin and hair, while the structure of the skull can help determine race. All this information can be fed into the Angelator to present a three-dimensional sketch of the subject. That image can then be shown to witnesses or run through a database to find a visual match.

Other Items

Oftentimes, items found inside or with the subject can be valuable aids in victim identification. Medical apparatus, such as hearing aids, pins, and implants usually carry serial numbers that can be tracked back to the doctor who performed the operation. Those numbers can lead directly to the identity of the victim. Items found with the body, such as a wallet, plane tickets, or a personal memento can also help in identification. In Dr. Brennan's own personal case it was a silver belt buckle with a dolphin design that confirmed for her the identity of a skeleton as her mother ('The Woman in Limbo').

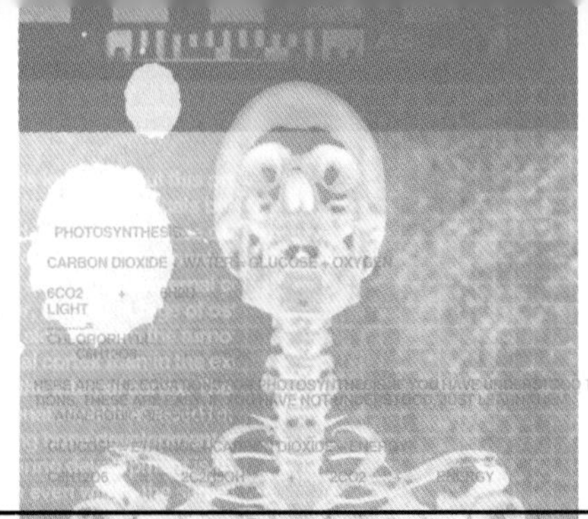

THE MAN IN THE WALL

WRITTEN BY ELIZABETH BENJAMIN DIRECTED BY TAWNIA MCKIERNAN

GUEST STARRING: MORRIS CHESTNUT (AGENT OAKES), BOKEEM WOODBINE (RANDALL HALL), ANNE DUDEK (TESSA JANKOW) CHARLES DUCKWORTH (RULZ), LAZ ALONSO (GEORGE WARREN), ROBERT GOSSETT (MR. TAYLOR)

- Mummified remains are found inside the walls of a nightclub. Metham-phetamine in the victim's lungs, nasal passages, and coating the alveoli in his lungs reveal that he died of asphyxiation. The dry air convection behind the wall removed the moisture from his body, which explains the condition of the remains.
- Low-density polyethylene residue from a plastic bag and metham-phetamine crystals are found in the victim's eyes. Damage to the inside of the victim's lip made by his own teeth, implies that someone smothered him with the bag of meth.
- Dr. Brennan rehydrates the victim's hand and slips the skin over her own to obtain a fingerprint. The print identifies the body as Roy Taylor, a popular rapper known as DJ Mount.
- An odd indentation, initially suspected to be genetic, is found on the victim's skull.
- A second body is discovered under the floor of a new recording studio. Dental records confirm that it is Eve Warren, the victim's girlfriend. Insect activity suggests she died at the same time as her boyfriend, while other indicators confirm the manner of death was also the same. She has a similar indentation on the **manubrium**, proving the "dimple" is not genetic.
- The strange marks on the victims are matched to the metal end of a cane carried by suspect Randall Hall.

Angela finally convinces Brennan to go out clubbing with her and have some fun, but Bones almost causes a riot with her analytical analysis of the "tribal" music. When she pushes an irate attacker through a wall, a mummified body is revealed, along with a shower of meth that rains down on the club. Booth arrives with a team of investigators and his girlfriend, Tessa, in tow.

While working the case, Booth is also preparing for a Jamaican vacation with Tessa. This would be the first extended vacation for the couple, which Angela accidentally sabotages by raising quest-ions about what it means for their relationship. When Angela hears that the trip is cancelled, she assumes both Booth and Tessa balked out of fear of the commitment it implied. It turns out, however, it was Tessa who cancelled the trip and likely ended the relationship.

Bones was always intended to be equal parts comedy and drama. 'The Man in the Wall' provided many light touches amid the serious crime – particularly one scene that can only be described as comic gold. After Brennan throws someone through the nightclub wall, a cloud of meth explodes on the club-goers, including her and Angela. By the time Booth arrives, both women are high as proverbial kites in a scene that Emily Deschanel recalls as one of her favorites to play.

"You have to try to get into the feeling of what a drug like that is," Deschanel explains. "I've never done that drug, so I don't know. I read about how it makes you feel and tried to emulate that. There's a lot of humor in there too. It was a lot of fun. It's funny, as you even start feeling a little high when you do it because you're constantly thinking in

Hodgins: How many times do you want me to poke Zack?

Brennan: Just once but as hard as you can.

Zack: As hard as he can? Why don't I hit him as hard as I can?

Hodgins: Because you have arms like noodles, while I am vigorous and burly.

that way and getting your mind into that state."

The episode is also notable because it's the first time Angela gets her best friend out on the town. The friendship between the empiricist and the free spirit is integral to the series and to Brennan's character, especially. "I think it brings so much," says Deschanel. "You look at Brennan who has really shut off her emotions for a long time and is kind of scared to feel. I think people seek opposites to balance themselves out in the world; you kind of want to balance out whatever extreme you go to, and that's a natural occurrence. You'd probably find a lot of models like that in science."

True to her character, Michaela Conlin agrees with Deschanel without bringing up any scientific comparisons. She explains how friendships have developed among the entire cast. "I remember the first day I met Emily, I was like, 'I can't believe I get to be this girl's friend.' She's a wonderful person, so it's really, really nice to not have to fake it. We've all become so close that it's really like a crazy family – we spend more time with each other than we do our own families. We laugh all day long."

Manubrium: The upper part of the sternum where the clavicle and the first two ribs articulate.

'Rize' by Flii Stylz, *Rize*
'Soul Survivor' by Young Jeezy (featuring Akon), *Let's Get It: Thug Motivation 101*
'Run It' by Chris Brown, *Chris Brown*
'Something' by Cary Brothers, *Waiting for Your Letter*
'Gunpowder Language' by move.meant, *The Good Money EP*

THE MAN ON DEATH ROW

WRITTEN BY NOAH HAWLEY DIRECTED BY DAVID JONES

GUEST STARRING: RACHELLE LAFEVRE (AMY MORTON), MICHAEL MANTELL (LARRY CARLYLE), EDWARD EDWARDS (DAVID ROSS), DAN GILVEZAN (MR. WRIGHT), TERRI CAVANAUGH (MRS. WRIGHT), HEAVY D. (SID SHAPIRO), HEATH FREEMAN (HOWARD EPPS), MICHAEL ROTHHAAR (JUDGE COHEN)

While Brennan is at FBI headquarters making a (twice denied) formal request to carry a gun, defense attorney Amy Morton interrupts to request Booth's assistance in reopening the Howard Epps case. Booth reluctantly agrees to reexamine the evidence in the case of the death-row inmate, if only to confirm to himself that the right man is about to die. As the clock ticks down to the execution, Brennan finds enough questions from the initial autopsy to request an exhumation of the body, an act with which Booth strongly disagrees. When the investigation turns up two additional bodies, Epps is the primary suspect in their murders. This prompts a stay in the execution for the FBI to investigate the new cases. In the end, the murderer gets exactly what he had wanted – to live and possibly cause more harm in the future.

As the team works on the case, Angela is pulled in on her night off. She makes the mistake of bringing her date by the office. When he sees her working on the remains of the exhumed body – a job description difficult to explain in an online personal ad – he's horrified by what she does for a living and abruptly ends the date.

'The Man on Death Row' marks the first in a trilogy of episodes about serial killer Howard Epps that play out over the first two seasons of *Bones*. "The network and studio have certain demands," admits creator/executive producer Hart Hanson. "They say, 'Do a serial killer story' – but I don't like serial killers. They've been very successful for us because we do them, but we do them in our way."

Hanson's concern about a serial killer story is that the guest character can overwhelm the episode and take too much attention away from the core characters. Though every episode of *Bones* revolves around a mystery, the focal point of the show is the relationships between the characters. "It's the smaller moments, those are the places where it really comes down to the story and the actors," says co-executive

Brennan: I'll ask the others, but they might have plans.

Booth: It's Friday night and they're racing beetles.

- At the personal request of Special Agent Booth, files on murder victim April Wright are reexamined on the eve of the execution of her convicted killer, Howard Epps.
- The original ME had concluded that particles lodged between the left **triquetral** and the **capitate** were bone fragments dislodged by the tire iron used in the attack. However, radiographic shadows on the X-ray are too opaque for bone.
- A shard of bone with traces of aggregate gravel is found on the victim's clothes. It was missed in the initial autopsy and could indicate the body was moved from the original murder scene. Dr. Brennan decides that the body needs to be exhumed to further examine the evidence.
- Post-exhumation, several pieces of formed material are found lodged in the bones of the body, signifying that the body was dragged through gravel after the attack.
- Slivers of metal, silt and pollen are found in the skull fractures. The pollen is from **spartina alterniflora**, which is only found along the Chesapeake Bay. The silt contains complex chemicals, indicating that the victim was killed in a marsh near a chemical plant. The weapon is located near the Rock Hall Processing Plant, along with the remains of two other young girls.

producer Steve Beers. "Those emotional moments.Those are the moments that really get you. One of the fun things in my job is to be able to quietly sit in a corner and watch those moments."

To provide those great moments in the larger serial killer storyline, the intelligent psychopath, Howard Epps, will develop an obsession with Dr. Brennan. This fixation will affect both her and Booth deeply in the follow up episodes 'The Blonde in the Game' and 'The Man in the Cell'.

This story also differs from the traditional *Bones* episode as it introduces a very literal ticking clock element to heighten suspense. As the squints work to possibly prove the condemned man innocent, the audience watches as a digital display pops onscreen from time to time showing the countdown to his execution. The effect is used to draw in the viewers as the characters race against time, only to suffer the horrible irony of saving the killer's life by proving he's murdered others.

Triquetral: A pyramid-shaped bone in the wrist.

Capitate: Largest of the carpal bones, located in the center of the wrist.

Spartina alterniflora: Commonly known as smooth cordgrass and usually found in salt marshes.

THE GIRL IN THE FRIDGE

WRITTEN BY DANA COEN DIRECTED BY SANFORD BOOKSTAVER

GUEST STARRING: JOSH HOPKINS (MICHAEL STIRES), MATT ROSS (NEIL MEREDITH), ALICIA COPPOLA (JOY DEAVER), LEONARD ROBERTS (D.A. ANDREW LEVITT), RACHEL MINER (MARY COSTELLO), ROSS MCCALL (SCOTT COSTELLO), KATE MCNEIL (AUDREY SCHILLING), LOU RICHARDS (DR. BARRAGAN)

Dr. Brennan's former professor (and former lover), Michael Stires, shows up at the Jeffersonian, and at the same time Booth arrives with a refrigerator housing the decomposing body of a missing teen. While the team gets to work on the remains, Brennan takes a rare night off to rekindle her relationship with Stires.

At the Jeffersonian, Brennan uses the evidence to show up her mentor by proving that the victim had been bound while her captors kept upping her intake of drugs to combat her pain, until she died of an overdose. Stires yields to his student's expertise, but later challenges it in court when he takes a role as an expert witness for the defense.

The D.A.'s jury consultant expresses concern over Brennan's overly technical explanations; while Stires manages to poke enough holes in their case that it looks like the defendants might escape prosecution.

Brennan continues her dry testimony until the D.A. – at Booth's suggestion – brings her personal family history into the case. This allows Brennan to access her emotions and present an explanation that the jury can absorb. Though the ploy works, Brennan is upset with Booth for putting her private life on display. She is able to move past it as they begin work on their next case: a body found on the scaffolding surrounding the Washington Monument.

When looking for the perfect setting for the show executive producer Barry Josephson explains that they needed somewhere with an international flavor, so Washington D.C. fitted the bill perfectly. Plus it was ideal in terms of plots, since it's also the home of the FBI, CIA, and Interpol. "Any kind of case could come in and out of D.C.," notes Josephson, "so I thought basing the institution there was a smart move."

Brennan: ...I'm sorry if that's difficult for you to understand. But what we have isn't traditional.

Angela: Don't talk to me about traditional, okay? I've dated circus people.

- A refrigerator containing the partially liquified remains of a decomposed human skeleton is found in a ravine and brought to the Jeffersonian for examination. Dental records indicate the victim is missing person Maggie Schilling.
- Marks found on the kitchen floor of suspects Mary and Scott Costello match the refrigerator.
- Chemical analysis of the victim's liver and kidney tissues shows significant evidence of a fatal dose of the narcotic **hydromorphone**.
- Both the victim's wrists show signs of stress fractures. X-rays reveal the victim has a low bone density; the parathyroid hormone levels are also low. The victim's medical records indicate that she suffered from **hyperparathyroidism**.
- A pair of fur-lined handcuffs are found among the suspects' belongings. Strands of matching fur are found embedded in the bones of the victim's wrists.
- Marks on the left and right medial **malleoli** suggest that the victim's legs were bound. These marks are believed to be erosion patterns from the bones rubbing together over time. There is also evidence of inflammation on her right **humerus** and **ilium**. The bone abnormalities were caused from lying in one position for a long time.

However, just because the Jeffersonian is based there does not mean that the production is. The Washington D.C. locations are usually stock footage or second unit, meaning a production crew – minus the actors – visits the city to film locations. Those locations can then be cut into an episode as an establishing shot, added into a background with CGI, or seen out of the windows of Booth's SUV as he drives through the city.

The actual location filming in Los Angeles does present its share of challenges. Not the least of which, says Hart Hanson, is having to disguise the distinctive features of the west coast, "It's a nightmare trying to hide palm trees and desert," he explains.

'The Girl in the Fridge' ends with a memorable shot of Booth and Brennan on a scaffolding as the camera pulls back to reveal them midway to the top of the Washington Monument. "That was something," recalls Hanson. "We had to fight with the studio because they thought it was going to cost a fortune – but it didn't. The little chunk that they were standing on was built onstage out of nothing, just some scaffolding and a white wall. The two of them were sitting there with fans going to blow their hair. And then as you pulled back, the green screen CGI kicked in and it was great."

Hydromorphone: Hospital heroin. A drug used to relieve moderate to severe pain.

Hyperparathyroidism: A condition in which overactive parathyroid glands produce an abnormally high level of parathyroid hormone in the body.

Malleoli: The bone protuberance on either side of the ankle.

Humerus: The long bone of the upper arm.

Ilium: Upper portion of the pelvis.

'Hold Tight' by Mark Geary, Ghosts

THE MAN IN THE FALLOUT SHELTER

WRITTEN BY HART HANSON DIRECTED BY GREG YAITANES

GUEST STARRING: JIM ORTLIEB (HAL), HEAVY D. (SID SHAPIRO), MARGARET AVERY (IVY GILLESPIE), BILLY GIBBONS (ANGELA'S DAD)

- A skeleton is discovered in a fallout shelter dating back to the 1950s. A .22 caliber slug found in the skull matches the gun the man was holding, implying he committed suicide.
- Zack attempts to obtain a core sample from the bones, this releases the **coccidioidomycosis** pathogen into the air, forcing the lab into lockdown.
- Two tickets to Paris and a wedding band are found in the victim's clothing, along with a compass, a penknife, and some coins. Labels in the man's suit are from a local tailor shop which the squints discover is still in operation. The shop's records indicate that the man's name was Lionel Little.
- Letters found in the suitcase are linked to a woman named Ivy, who was reportedly the last person to see Lionel alive. The letters suggest that the African American woman was pregnant.
- Traces of lead and nickel in the **osteological profile** suggest that he was a coin collector. Among the change in his pocket is a 1943 bronze one-cent piece. Current value: over $100,000.
- Records reveal that the building where the body was found was originally a house owned by a man named Gil Adkins, who was known for fencing jewels and stolen art. It is believed that Adkins killed the victim for his coin collection, though he missed the coin with the highest value.

Dr. Brennan welcomes a distraction from the annual Jeffersonian Christmas party with the arrival of a mystery from the fifties. When a pathogen in the bone dust from the victim sets off an alarm, the team is quarantined and they have no choice but to remain in lockdown through Christmas. Booth is especially upset to miss out on spending the holiday with his son.

Brennan is determined to solve the mystery and keep her mind off the anniversary of her parents' disappearance. The rest of the group, however, does take a break from the investigation to receive visits from their loved ones.

The team uncovers the life of the victim and learns that the woman he left behind is still living under the impression that he abandoned her and their unborn child. Brennan meets with the woman gifting her with the coin that will pay for her granddaughter's education and reuniting a family.

"The network said they wanted a Christmas-themed episode," recalls Hart Hanson. "And we really needed a bottle show. We really, really, needed a bottle show." A "bottle show" is an episode that takes place exclusively on the existing sets so the production doesn't need to budget for new sets. "It actually turned out to be one of our most expensive shows," Hanson admits. "The bottle show thing didn't work out!"

"The first season, like any first season, you're pressed financially. You don't have anything," explains co-executive producer Steve Beers. "Everything is for the first time. Every piece of wardrobe, every wall, everything has to be bought the first time. So financially first seasons are extremely challenging. We promised that we'd do a bottle show to get closer to what the budget number for the season was supposed to be. We wrote a bottle show, but it was filmically so interesting that, by the time we added up the cost, it was as expensive as

Brennan: Anthropologically speaking, gifts are a way of asserting dominance in a group. Now imagine an entire holiday devoted to self-promotion, and especially in this materialistic culture. How can you expect me to get behind that? How can you get behind it?

Booth: Wow, that's deep. It's a very deep pile of crap.

anything else we ever did." The trade off, however, was that the episode became one of the most popular of the show's first two seasons.

Writing the episode had its own inherent challenges that had nothing to do with the budget. Hanson recalls enjoying confronting Brennan and Booth's very different views on religion. "How do you do a Christmas show without touching upon what Brennan calls 'The Christ Myth'? Some of the fun in there was figuring out where everyone was on the line of religiosity," he notes. "Especially with Booth being a religious man in his heart, and Brennan being a complete empiricist. I thought it was a lot of fun at the Chinese food dinner for Brennan to find out that they weren't all with her and Booth wasn't alone in his views. She was completely shocked!"

"I loved that episode," enthuses Michaela Conlin. "I love that we were all working together within this one space. That Hart wrote it and that Greg [Yaitanes] directed it, as he directed our pilot. It was just all of us coming back together. That was at a really great time in the series. It was just at the halfway point of season one, so it was a really unifying experience for all of us to work together for eight days solid. It was a blast."

Coccidioidomycosis: Valley Fever. A potentially fatal respiratory disease caused by the inhalation of spores from a fungus.

Osteological profile: Analysis of the skeletal bones.

'Have Yourself a Merry Little Christmas' by Tori Amos, *Spark*

'Winter Wonderland' by Jewel, *Joy: A Holiday Collection*

'Let it Snow, Let it Snow, Let it Snow' by Brian Setzer, *Dig that Crazy Christmas*

THE WOMAN AT THE AIRPORT

WRITTEN BY TERESA LIN DIRECTED BY GREG YAITANES

GUEST STARRING: CLAIRE COFFEE (SPECIAL AGENT TRICIA FINN), HARRY GROENER (DR. HENRY ATLAS), MICHAEL B. SILVER (DR. ANTON KOSTOV), MARIKA DOMINCZYK (LESLIE SNOW), NATALIJA NOGULICH (IVANA BARDU), JANN CARL (HERSELF), ADAM GRIMES (NICK HUDSON), MCNALLY SAGAL (MARTINA SIKES), PENNY MARSHALL (HERSELF)

- A woman's mangled remains are found on the beach adjacent to L.A. International Airport. The architecture of the skull had been radically altered through extensive and invasive plastic surgery, which hinders attempts at identification.
- X-rays show two dark masses near the pelvis that turn out to be breast implants. Serial numbers on the implants initially prove useless for identification as they had been reported stolen six months previously. An implant from the same batch was reported as recovered from a local escort, who provides a possible ID on the victim.
- The victim's body shows evidence of stabbing — one strike to the sternum and two to the **costal cartilages**. By comparing the wounds to the marks left on the woman's jaw it is determined that the murder weapon was a medical instrument used in an extremely rare cosmetic surgical procedure.
- **E-glass fibers** found on the victim signify that she was on a boat shortly before her death.
- A fingernail with a cubic zirconium stone embedded in it is also found on the victim. At first it was assumed to be the victim's, but it proved to belong to the murderer, her friend and fellow escort Leslie Snow.

Booth hijacks Brennan and takes her to Los Angeles to investigate a body found at LAX. The victim had put herself through such dramatic cosmetic surgery that a definitive identification is impossible. Brennan is particularly upset to see the lengths the woman had gone to, obliterating her true self by altering her body, to try to meet some unattainable perfection. Booth and Brennan succeed in identifying the woman and return her remains to her family. Before they wrap the case, though, Brennan has time to meet with a producer interested in making her book into a film.

Meanwhile, back at the lab, Dr. Goodman works with the squints to authenticate the remains of what is believed to be a skeleton from the Iron Age. Tensions run high between Goodman and Hodgins due to their divergent approaches to the work. Finally they unite with a plausible explanation of why they cannot authenticate the remains at this time.

"I thought 'The Woman at the Airport' was a great Booth and Brennan episode," notes executive producer Barry Josephson. "The story really defined their characters. We always try to make that balance happen: where the show explores the characters, as well as solving a really intriguing case." This episode explores Brennan's deeply emotional reaction to someone altering their very bones for the sake of 'beauty'. At the same time we learn how important the FBI is to Booth when he berates the L.A.-based federal agent for using the Bureau as a stepping-stone in her film career.

Once again an episode takes Booth and Brennan outside of Washington, which was one of the goals of the series from the start. "I think it's very

Brennan: ...These bones you bring me, I give them a face. I say their names out loud. I return them to their loved ones. And you arrest the bad guy. I like that.

Booth: So do I.

important for her to travel all over the United States because that's what forensic anthropologists actually do," Josephson explains. "People wait for the expert to come to them, and the expert comes. A great thing in 'The Man in the Bear' was that she was shipping body parts back to the lab. She did the same thing in this episode. She set up her own little lab in L.A. to do some markings on the bones and figure out how things would have been. I think that getting her out in the field was very, very important." The added bonus with this episode was that the story called for them to explore L.A., the city in which the show is filmed. For once, they could go out on the street and not have to hide the palm trees.

In this episode, like in others, we see the flipside of Brennan's arrangement with Booth to be involved in the fieldwork. Though she insists on being an integral part of the investigations, she balks at traveling such a long distance because it takes her away from the lab. The conflict fieldwork represents is one of the difficulties Brennan shares with her counterpart from Kathy Reichs' novels. "That was in Kathy's books," Josephson confirms. "For that character, her deal was 'I'm going out into the field.' And her coping mechanism was, 'If I am – every single day – just dealing with remains, I will not survive this gig.' It's the same deal you see Brennan make with Booth in the pilot episode."

Costal cartilages: Bars of transparent cartilage that connect the sternum and the ends of the ribs.
E-glass fibers: Marine fiberglass

'Ooh La La' by Goldfrapp, *Number 1*
'Precious' by Depeche Mode, *Playing the Angel*
'Show Your Style' by Ferry Corsten, *Right of Way*
'Free Los Angeles' by Baby, *Baby*
'I'm Slipping Away' by Messy

THE WOMAN IN THE CAR

WRITTEN BY NOAH HAWLEY DIRECTED BY DWIGHT LITTLE

GUEST STARRING: ZELJKO IVANEK (CARL DECKER), SUZANNE CRYER (AGENT PICKERING), LAWRENCE PRESSMAN (TRENT SEWARD), JAKE CHERRY (DONOVAN DECKER), JAIME RAY NEWMAN (STACY GOODYEAR), SARAH ANN SCHULTZ (MARIA SEMOV), ALEXA FISCHER (SHARON POMEROY), JOHN M. JACKSON (FBI DEPUTY DIRECTOR SAM CULLEN)

- A victim in a vehicle fire is identified as Polina Rozalina Sernov, mother of eight year-old Donovan Dimitri Decker and recently separated from Carl Decker. A burned backpack and lone sneaker suggest that her child was kidnapped.
- A piece of cartilage found lodged in the victim's larynx is identified as **antihelix**, indicating that she bit off the ear of her attacker before her death. Particulates in the accompanying earwax are identified as the pollen of **eragrostis curvula**. Traces of automotive grade asbestos from brake pads are also present.
- Broken teeth, bilateral fractures in the **femoral necks** and in the **proximal humeral heads**, and clots in the victim's lungs reveal that she was electrocuted prior to her death in a manner that implies torture.
- The child's severed finger is sent to investigators as a warning. Blood saturation levels in the surrounding tissues are high, meaning he was alive at the time of the amputation. Traces of lead and methyl tertiary butyl ether on the bone suggest the boy is being held at an abandoned gas station.
- Investigators use the signal from the murder victim's cell phone to triangulate the location to a seventy-five square mile area that has six abandoned gas stations, which leads them to the missing child.

Another case involving a child motivates the team in a personal way as they race to locate the missing boy. The suspicion is that the boy was kidnapped and his mother killed to stop the child's father, Carl Decker, from testifying to a grand jury against the corporation for which he once worked. Complications ensue when Booth and Brennan are forced to work around the U.S. Marshals, who have been told to keep Decker, who is in witness protection, in the dark about the recent events. Once they locate the boy and reunite him with his father, it is left to the grand jury to determine if the mercenaries involved in the kidnapping and murder had been hired by the company Decker was testifying against.

A state department employee arrives to interview the Jeffersonian staff and evaluate their security clearance for working on classified cases. The squints react differently to the interviews, with Hodgins upset that he doesn't pose a viable threat as a political instigator and Brennan concerned to learn that her interviewer has a lower security rating than she does herself.

The B-plot in which the state department agent interviews the squints provides a lot of comic fodder for the episode. As ever, the characters react in their own unique ways. For Angela it becomes like a therapy session, while Zack's interview turns into a convoluted roundabout on the

Pickering: What I need to do here is to establish that you are not a threat to the security of this country.

Zack: I'm getting a degree in forensic anthropology. I'm half way through another in engineering. What are you afraid I will do? Build a race of criminal robots that will destroy the earth?

Pickering: Do you have that kind of fantasy often?

Zack: Very often.

nature of secret information. But it is Hodgins' reaction to not being interviewed that provides the most insight into his character.

When Hodgins learns that he's already been checked out and deemed harmless, he is immediately insulted. He believes that the conspiracy theories he's been weaving would have at least earned him a spot on some government watch list. Not that TJ Thyne thinks his character really believes his thoughts are that extreme. "Some call him a conspiracy theorist," Thyne says. "He would say he's a realist."

The series skillfully manages to mesh this comic subplot with a story about a murdered mother and her missing child. The comic factor is something the producers feel has a counterpart in life and they have determined it to be an essential aspect of the series.

Co-executive producer Steve Beers is a television veteran, with his fair share of crime dramas under his belt. "I've done police shows and a lot of different things over the years and so I've been to visit morgues and crime sites and so on. I've found that when you're around death all the time, you have to normalize it in some way. We wanted to put that sense into the show. That factor allows us to make those turns on a dime, moving quickly from something dark to something humorous. Just within the structure of telling a story, the actors and their characters are so strong that they can make the moves asked of them by the writers and they just make it seamless."

Antihelix: A ridge of cartilage found behind the folded edge of the outer ear.
Eragrostis curvula: Weeping love grass, traditionally found in South Africa.
Femoral neck: The area just below the ball-and-socket hip joint.
Proximal humeral head: The uppermost part of the humerus.

AUTOPSY REPORT

JEFFERSONIAN INSTITUTE

Report No.	Date of Examined.
Subject. The Angelator	

The Angelator is a computer-imaging unit that accepts a full array of digital input, processes it, and then projects it as a three-dimensional holographic image. It was developed by Angela Montenegro (patent pending). The Angelator's primary function is for facial reconstruction and victim identification, though it is also used for crime scene reenactment, wound examination – and it can make lovely holiday decorations.

Facial Reconstruction

A clean skull is taken and a nearly perfect three-dimensional model of a subject's head and face is created for identification purposes. Tissue markers are placed along the contours of the skull to suggest depth of skin and then the information is fed into the Angelator to create a face. Estimates are made for hair, eye color, and other physical traits based on any information known about the victim. The end result is a three-dimensional version of the victim's head and face that can be used for a visual identification or run through missing persons files to obtain a match.

Example: In the case of Cleo Louise Eller ('Pilot'), the skull was badly damaged, but Dr. Brennan managed the reconstruction and applied the tissue markers. The information was fed into the Angelator and a three-dimensional recreation of the victim was projected in the imaging unit. Racial

indicators, such as cheekbone dimensions, nasal arch, and occipital measurement suggested the victim was African American. Estimates were made on skin tone for an African American, a Caucasian, and a woman of mixed race. Visual identification was immediate.

Wounds and Weapons

The Angelator can also be used to examine wound patterns and compare them to weapons fed into the system to match the instrument to the damage it left behind. The size, shape and depth of a wound can indicate not only the type of weapon used, but also the size and relative strength of the attacker and the angle of attack.

Example: In the case of Warren Granger ('The Superhero in the Alley'), the victim's spinal cord was severed by something sharp, but the wound did not match a knife. Considering the victim was a graphic novelist, the fictional weaponry from his comic book was fed into the computer and the weapons were compared to the wound pattern – there were no matches. However, the visual rendering of the wound allowed Booth to determine that the weapon was a bevel knife: a triangular three-sided blade used to clean bowling balls.

Crime Scene Recreations

Recreations are a particular highlight of the Angelator's abilities. All information gathered from the examination of a body can be fed into the computer to design a model of the victim prior to an attack. Taking that information, various scenarios can be run to determine exactly how the victim died and help identify the attacker or confirm the identity of a suspect.

Example: In a case in which the victim was initially believed to be Warren Lynch (in the season two première 'The Titan on the Tracks') a crime scene recreation provided an integral clue to the mystery. The victim's shoulder and elbow were dislocated post-mortem. Based on the angle of the bones, a simulation of the motion that caused the dislocation was projected on the Angelator. The motion best resembled that of a man putting his arm through the sleeve of a jacket. This indicated that corpse was dressed to look like the presumed victim, Warren Lynch, signifying that the man's death was purposely staged.

Subject.

Behind the scenes with the Angelator

The Angelator is one of the key visual components contributing to the uniqueness of *Bones*, and helps set it apart from other forensics shows on television. But more than just helping with the look of the show, it was integral in the creation of one of the characters. Barry Josephson recalls its incarnation: "When Hart and I first conceived of the Angelator and what Angela's character did, I had ripped out of the newspaper this 3-D projection from a museum, this holographic thing. It looked brilliant."

Their research had already shown what facial reconstruction artists could do with clay models, maquette sculptures, and art renderings. They'd learned how people recreated faces and identities from the skeletal remains. "It was just brilliant artistic work," Josephson adds. "And Angela's character came flying out of Hart, seeing this and looking at Kathy's books. It was really interesting watching him create each one of these characters based on the work they would be doing." Together that artwork was merged with the technology and both the character and the Angelator emerged.

Angela's alter ego, Michaela Conlin, agrees with Josephson's assessment of Angela's work: "I think her job is so interesting," says Conlin. "That she takes these bones and says, 'All right, who was this?' and then identifies them and gives them faces, is really cool."

It should come as no surprise that the actors aren't really looking at three-dimensional holograms when they're filming a scene. They are working with little pieces of tape tied to a string where the holograms will be once they're added in post-production. "It's sort of crazy to not really be looking at anything when you're taping it," says Conlin. "It's a pretty fun challenge. Our wonderful technicians, who create those images and do everything on the computers, usually come in and describe to us what it's going to look like. They give us the height and width so we have an idea, but we really don't know until we watch it later what we're looking at. So you end up sort of looking cross-eyed at the person across from you."

The filming of the scene is only part of the process, associate producer David Jeffrey explains: "When it comes to creating an Angelator image, we have several meetings to discuss it. If the victim was hit on the back of the skull, often we'll start with the torso up and we'll show the skull. The creation you'll see is part of the skin and the skull. If we have to show the back of the skull then we'll focus in on that part of the skull, and we'll eliminate the rest of the torso and so forth. This way we can help focus the story."

The Angelator really showed off its skills in season one's 'The Woman in the Garden'. Jeffrey recalls, "That show was a special case in terms of the Angelator template. It dealt with a maid who fell from a ladder and banged her head against a bedpost. That scene was only three pages long but it was the first time in the history of *Bones* that we had to take the Angelator in the direction where we really had to create this crime in 3-D."

THE SUPERHERO IN THE ALLEY

WRITTEN BY ELIZABETH BENJAMIN DIRECTED BY JAMES WHITMORE JR.

GUEST STARRING: JUDITH HOAG (HELEN GRANGER), IVAR BROGGER (JOHN KELTON), AARON PAUL (STEW ELLIS), JOSH KEATON (JEREMY KUZNETSKY), ADRIANA DEMEO (ABIGAIL ZEALEY), JOHN MESE (TED MCGRUDER), SARAH ALDRICH (LUCY MCGRUDER), JOHN M. JACKSON (FBI DEPUTY DIRECTOR SAM CULLEN)

- Skeletal remains of a young man dressed in a costume are found in an alley. Dental records identify the deceased as seventeen year-old Warren Granger. Subsequent tests reveal the victim had **acute leukemia.**
- A bag found beside the body contains cellulose degraded from bodily tissues and decomposing fat. It is determined to be a graphic novel.
- Cause of death is a severed spinal cord. The victim's face and cranial vault are badly fractured. Blows to the **parietal bone** sent radiating fracture lines between the mid-frontal and anterior temporal buttresses, suggesting that the victim was killed in a brutal assault and then thrown from a building after his death.
- An extra piece of bone from the humerus is lodged in the victim's neck. It likely belonged to his attacker and was transferred by the weapon used in the fight. DNA tests indicate that the bone chip is from a male in his mid-thirties.
- Based on examination of the wound, the victim was killed by a weapon resembling a triangular three-sided knife. Booth realizes that the weapon must be a bevel knife — used in bowling alleys, such as the one where the victim worked, to clean bowling balls. The murderer is identified as the victim's boss.

Media pressure bumps a local murder case to FBI level after a group of sixth-grade students finds the body of a boy dressed in a superhero costume in an alley. The shy adolescent victim lived an isolated life writing himself as the superhero in his own comic books. A casual remark Booth makes about Brennan's similarities to the boy concerns her. She worries that she, too, lives an isolated life. Booth, however, reassures her that in many ways she is a superhero using her superior skills to solve crimes.

The victim also proved to be a hero. Knowing that he was dying of cancer, Warren gave his life in an attempt to protect a woman from her abusive husband. In an act of closure, Angela completes the boy's comic book and places it with his coffin at his funeral.

The challenge in creating a weekly procedural series centering on an FBI agent is finding reasons to raise a murder case to a federal profile. Sometimes, the reasoning is clearly defined, such as when the crime crosses state lines or a missing child is involved. Other times, it can be somewhat more nebulous, such as in the case of 'The Superhero in the Alley'. Booth becomes involved largely because it's high profile, with a lot of media attention putting pressure on the local police.

It's not out of the ordinary in the real world for the FBI to be welcomed into local investigations, but it's something the writers make sure they address. Technical advisor Mike Grasso is the

Booth: Ah, he has Batman number 127 featuring The Hammer of the Thor. This is worth about three hundred bucks.

Brennan: Booth, are you a nerd?

Booth: First of all, you mean geek and no, I'm not, okay? It's quite normal for an American male to read comic books.

man they look to for a plausible explanation. "When they come up with a good story, one of the biggest questions always is: 'Okay, Mike, how do we make this a federal case?' So that's why you find for example the body being found in a federal park or on a federal highway. Or at the airport." This concept led to episodes like 'The Woman at the Airport' and 'The Man with the Bone'.

"Sometimes you find a really good story and it doesn't come from Booth, it comes from Brennan instead," Grasso adds, citing the deeply personal story of 'The Skull in the Desert' that Brennan brings Booth in on. "Such as when a local jurisdiction that finds a body calls the Jeffersonian for assistance; and when they call the Jeffersonian, they're really calling Brennan – but then Booth goes along with her to help out because they're partners. And then, of course, the locals say, 'Yeah, we'll take any help you can give us.' So the FBI assists. Which is what the FBI normally does. That's the big thing – the FBI is kind of like a big brother that helps out. They really don't do a lot of stuff all on their own – other than terrorism. So, when they're called in, they're usually called in by jurisdictions that don't have the necessary resources, smaller jurisdictions. That's something that you see a lot."

Acute Leukemia: A form of cancer characterized by the rapid growth of immature blood cells.

Parietal bone: Bones located on either side of the skull that form part of the sides and roof of the skull.

'Feel it Now' by Black Rebel Motorcycle Club, *Howl*

'Bat Country' by Avenged Sevenfold, *City of Evil*

'Out of Control' by She Wants Revenge, *She Wants Revenge*

'Ah! Leah!' by Donny Iris, *Back on the Streets*

'Body Talk' by KIX, *Cool Kids*

THE WOMAN IN THE GARDEN

WRITTEN BY LAURA WOLNER *DIRECTED BY* SANFORD BOOKSTAVER

GUEST STARRING: MICHAEL CAVANAUGH (SENATOR ALAN CORMAN), DEY YOUNG (KATE CORMAN), MATT BARR (LOGAN CORMAN), ROBERT LASARDO (MIGUEL VILLEDA), JOSE PABLO CANTILLO (JOSE VARGAS), MIKE GOMEZ (HECTOR ALVAREDO), EMILIO RIVERA (RAMON ORTEZ), DENNIS COCKRUM (NEIL CLAYTON)

- The body of a woman is found in the trunk of a car. Decomposition, insect activity and **adipocere** in soil present with the body suggest she was buried for approximately six months prior to being removed from the ground.
- Cause of death was a single strike to the skull. Localized staining on the endocranial surface of the skull shows a **subdural hematoma**. Death was not instantaneous.
- Analysis of the soil reveals **fernaldia pandurata**, which leads to a search of a local garden and a second overturned grave.
- Genetic material from a **franklinia alatamaha** found on the shoe of the prime suspect leads to another garden, belonging to Senator Corman, where investigators find the missing second body — a male. Examination of the remains proves that he died of cancer.
- Both victims have holes in the sternum from a hereditary condition, signifying that they were related.
- The wood used in the weapon that killed the female victim matches a bedpost in the Senator's home. Dried blood and skin are found at the top of the post. A crime reenactment on the Angelator shows that the victim was pulled from a ladder before striking the post. The Senator's house manager is identified as the person who caused the accidental injury that led to her death.

A routine traffic stop requires the services of the FBI when a body is found in the trunk of a vehicle with out-of-state license plates. What begins as a case of Salvadoran gang-bangers in the barrio, ends up in the home of a prominent Senator with ties to El Salvador. It's revealed that the gang member – who is in the country illegally – simply wanted to bury his father and sister together. He had to move their bodies when the local garden was going to be razed for construction.

During the investigation, a gang leader places a hand on Brennan. He quickly learns that is a mistake when she defends herself with a few good blows, taking him down. The gang leader puts out a hit on her. When the FBI gang task force alerts Booth to this, he confronts the gang leader, quietly but firmly ensuring that he will stay away from Brennan.

As Chris Yagher explains, the process of creating the makeup effects for an episode of *Bones* starts, logically enough, with determining exactly what the producers and director want to see. "I read through the script and make a list of the possible makeup effects that I find. This list includes the episode's victim, or victims, any prosthetics to be applied to the actors, and any special props that may relate to the effects."

For Yagher and his team, the list for 'The Woman in the Garden' looked like this: (1) A severely decomposed female body covered in adipocere, with a skull fracture, shoveled incisors, and a

Hodgins: Fieldwork! Cool! Do I get a gun?

Brennan: You... you can't arm Hodgins and not me.

Booth: What is it with you people and the guns, huh?

sternal foramen. (2) An older, more skeletal male body also covered in adipocere, with a sternal foramen as well as a bullet in his hip. (3) A dried piece of skin on a bedpost. (4) Clean-bone versions of both bodies.

But that is only the beginning. Once Yagher has his prop list, he then comes up with a list of questions to ask the producers and the director to help clarify any ambiguities from the script. "I may ask such questions as: How much flesh remains on the bodies?" he explains. "What is the color of their hair? Do these bodies need to match any photos of the victims?"

After meeting with the producers and the director, he does the research that may help to solidify what the makeup effects should look like. "For instance, while researching details for 'The Woman in the Garden'," he clarifies, "I found pictures of bodies that contained adipocere, which is a whitish, waxy build-up that comes from the fat in a body. I also found reference photos of sternal foramen." Then, once all the questions are answered and the details are fleshed out, they can begin the actual construction of the makeup effects.

Adipocere: Grave wax. A substance consisting largely of fatty acids produced by chemical changes to body fat that occur after death.

Subdural hematoma: Traumatic brain injury in which blood collects between the dura and the arachnoid parts of the brain.

Fernaldia pandurata: Loroco buds. Loroco is an edible flowering plant found in El Salvador.

Franklinia alatamaha: A rare flowering plant that hasn't been seen in the wild since 1800.

'Nada Es Para Siempre' by Elefante, *Lo Que Andabamos Buscando*

'Rey De Reyes' by Sporty Loco, *Rey De Reyes*

THE MAN ON THE FAIRWAY

WRITTEN BY STEVE BLACKMAN DIRECTED BY TONY WHARMBY

GUEST STARRING: MICHAEL E. RODGERS (JESSE KANE), MICHAEL BOWEN (RAY SPARKS), SHASHAWNEE HALL (IAN DYSON), CHRISTINA CHAMBERS (KAREN ANDERSON)

- A private jet with five passengers on the manifest crashed on a local golf course, killing all the occupants and scattering their burnt remains. A sixth, unidentified victim on the VIP flight needs to be identified.
- Nasal ridges indicate the sixth passenger was a Caucasoid female approximately five-foot, ten-inches tall. A facial reconstruction is provided to investigators to compare against escort listings for a possible match.
- Three bone fragments found among the wreckage show no signs of charring, suggesting that they do not belong to any of the passengers.
- Rounded **supraorbital margins** among the unidentified bone fragments suggest the victim was male. Weathering discoloration indicates the bones had been on the golf course approximately five years.
- An osteological profile suggests post-mortem freezing, while distinctive marks on the bones indicate both a carving knife and a machine blade were used in dismembering the body. The conclusion is that the victim was frozen, dismembered, and fed into a wood chipper.
- An experiment is conducted to determine the dispersal pattern of the bone fragments, leading to the recovery of additional bone samples. A non-malignant bone tumor is found among the remains. It helps confirm the identity of the victim, which leads to the identity of the murderer.

When a private jet crashes on a golf course, Dr. Goodman, under pressure from the state department, places highest priority on determining the identity of a sixth passenger who is not listed on the manifest. The team, however, is much more interested in learning about the bone fragments found on the course that seem to have been there prior to the crash. Brennan calls Booth to help her investigate as she believes the bones belong to a murder victim. An expert on missing persons named Jesse Kane enters the picture, asking about the bone fragments. Jesse has been looking for his father for five years and believes that the bones may be his.

Because of her own missing parents, Brennan feels a kinship to the man missing his father, and so she secretly works the case, while the squints try to keep Dr. Goodman believing that identifying the sixth plane passenger is their priority. However, the bone fragments prove to be from an unrelated case.

Once the mystery is closed, Brennan shares the official file on her parents with Booth. She asks for his help in examining the evidence, since the official investigation went cold years earlier.

The episode opens with Dr. Brennan and Zack riding a cart through a golf course. Getting out of the lab may present its challenges to the production, but the actors really enjoy the opportunity. Zack's alter ego, actor Eric Millegan, is thrilled by the achievements of the *Bones* production team: "When we do go out I'm always amazed by the sets and the preparation that goes into it," he enthuses. "You know, it's just my job. I wake up at five in the morning, I have a map, I follow the directions and then get there and there's this huge plane-crash set. I'm like, 'Wow! That is crazy!' And this is my job."

In this case, Millegan was driving to a park by the water gap in Whittier, California that had already been used a few times in the series, due to the ease of access and the ability to create different looks there. "We've used that

Angela: [to Zack and Hodgins] Liars! You just wanted to see what happens when you toss a frozen pig into a wood-chipper!

for the coastline of Maryland," says co-executive producer Steve Beers with a laugh. "And we used it for the plane crash as a golf course because we couldn't shut down any golf courses. The golf courses around here don't want to stop play. We were going to need several days to put the plane in. So it wasn't even like we could come to them on a Monday and say, 'Can we have the course for half a day?' because of all the set dressing, which means laying the plane in and scarring the ground and then going back and repairing everything once we were done."

In the end, the producers realized that the easiest option was to create their own golf course. "So we'll go to where they'll let us do it," Beers continues. "We'll cut some grass, put a flag in and there's your golf course. That way you're able to open your lens up and not get hit by golf balls!"

Supraorbital margin: The bone directly under the eyebrow that creates the upper portion of the eye socket.

'Nothing Left to Lose' by Mat Kearny, *Nothing Left to Lose*

'Somewhere a Clock is Ticking' by Snow Patrol, *Final Straw*

'Look After You' by The Fray, *How to Save a Life*

TWO BODIES IN THE LAB

WRITTEN BY STEPHEN NATHAN **DIRECTED BY** ALLAN KROEKER

GUEST STARRING: ADAM BALDWIN (SPECIAL AGENT JAMIE KENTON), GREG ELLIS (KEVIN HOLLINGS), COBY RYAN MCLAUGHLIN (DAVID SIMMONS), RON MARASCO (LEWIS SLATER)

- Bones belonging to former mob boss James Cugini wash ashore in the Chesapeake Bay. Algae growth signifies the body had been in the bay for six years.
- Marks from bullet wounds in the sternum, arm and skull are revealed once the bones are clean. A computer recreation reverse engineers the marks in the wounds to recreate the bullet's **striation**, in an attempt to match the wounds to the weapon. Before a comparison can take place, the murderer, an FBI special agent assigned to the original case, confesses.
- A second body in an unrelated case is found in an abandoned warehouse having been tortured and ripped apart by dogs. Wounds to the body show that the victim was cut so the blood would attract the dogs. Her throat was also slashed by a pocketknife with a nick in the blade.
- Scrapings in the orbital cavity indicate that the victim's eyes were gouged out. The scrapings are rougher than the knife wounds and it is later determined that the marks were made from the crenulations of a key.
- Examining images of the keys from the suspect's large collection reveals a pattern that matches the grooves in the victim's bone. The murderer in the first case killed this suspect before he could be arrested.

Dr. Brennan's attempt at online dating starts out poorly when she's shot at on the way to her first date. It's possible the attempt on Brennan's life is related to the case she's working on: the murder of former mob boss, Jimmy Cugini. Or it could have something to do with another case where a victim was tortured and attacked by dogs. Both high profile cases could involve people trying to stop the forensic anthropologist from doing her job. Booth, however, is more than willing to believe that the culprit is the guy she met online.

Booth is injured in an explosion meant for Brennan and he's forced to leave her in the care of Special Agent Kenton, an original investigator on the Cugini case. When evidence suggests someone on the inside was behind the attacks on Brennan, Booth realizes that the clues point to Kenton. Booth checks himself out of hospital and rushes to Brennan's aid, stopping his fellow FBI agent before Kenton is able to take another victim.

Once upon a time, it was easy to tell the good guys from the bad. The good guys wore the white hats, while the bad guys went dark. Nowadays, the lines are a little more blurred, especially on television where shows like *The Shield* shine the spotlight on corrupt officers, and *The Sopranos* glorifies mobsters. As a series, *Bones* treats law enforcement agents with the utmost respect; though, on rare occasions, the writers do explore the darker side.

Police technical advisor Mike Grasso speculates that the writers' reluctance to deal with this darker side to law enforcement is due to their relationship with their advisors. "It's because they relate everything to their relationship with the guys that are helping them do the show," he reflects. "Sometimes I

Booth: ...an agent talked to a witness who saw a couple go into a building off North 23rd.

Hodgins: Just "a building"? Oh, yeah. That's real specific.

Booth: Well, crack-heads, you know, aren't that detail oriented.

scratch my head and go, 'You're going to make the bad guy the cop?' And they go, 'Yeah'. And I go, 'Okay, if you're going to make the bad guy the cop, then do this.' Basically, what we show is the fracture in the character, which is something real. They're great writers so it's interesting the way they explore the character. They bring out someone who is fed up, who can't deal with it any longer. Someone who has been doing the job for years and years and they can't go on – they just give up on it."

In this case, they created a character who was on the take while undercover in the mob. Kenton could justify killing Cugini because he was a bad guy, so in some sense his death ultimately made the world a better place. However, the need to cover up the murder forced his actions to snowball. Grasso is quick to point out that things like that don't happen every day in law enforcement. "When I discuss it with the writers, often we twist it and it's okay because it shows that there are good officers and that ninety-nine point nine-nine percent of them are squared away good guys. But like everything else, there are some that go wrong."

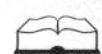

Striation: A thin narrow groove in the surface of an item — in this case, a bullet. By creating a ballistic fingerprint from a bullet's striation, it is possible to match the barrel of the gun that fired that bullet.

'Hot Blooded' by Foreigner, *Complete Greatest Hits*
'Walking on Moonlight' by Brookville, *Wonderfully Nothing*
'A Pain That I'm Used To' by Depeche Mode

THE WOMAN IN THE TUNNEL

WRITTEN BY STEVE BLACKMAN & GREG BALL
DIRECTED BY JOE NAPOLITANO

GUEST STARRING: GLENN PLUMMER (HAROLD OVERMEYER), MARY MARA (HELEN BRONSON), DAVID DENMAN (PHIL GARFIELD), BRIAN GROSS (KYLE MONTROSE), RYAN ALOSIO (DUKE DIALLEL), KEITH PILLOW (MICHAEL PRESTON)

- A woman's remains are found at the bottom of an airshaft in the tunnels beneath D.C. The serial number on a pin in her knee is matched to documentary filmmaker, Marni Hunter. Her fiancé had reported her missing ten days earlier.
- The victim fell approximately forty feet, landing feet first and crushing her **tibia** and **fibula**. Her skull also suffered traumatic injuries inconsistent with that type of fall.
- Damage to the left side of her skull is in a fracture pattern consistent with a sharp, pointed weapon. The entry point of the injury has a distinctive T-shape, which matches a Hanks climbing axe.
- During the investigation, it is discovered that the victim had been in possession of an official vault seal manufactured by the War Office. The vault it belonged to was thought to be one of the lost vaults housing cultural treasures from U.S. history.
- The victim's clothing shows traces of diamond dust from an older tunnel, indicating that she had been moved after her death. By entering all the modern and historical city plans, including ventilation shafts and tunnels, into the Angelator and using the collected information from the case, the team is able to pinpoint the location of the vault. There, Brennan and Booth find the murderers looting the treasure.

The body of a woman is found in the maze-like tunnels beneath Washington, D.C. Rats attacking the body pose a problem until Brennan borrows Booth's gun to fire on the rats and move them away. In the tunnels, Brennan and Booth stumble across an underground city, populated by people who live a separate life from the surface world. At first, these people and their odd lifestyle make their leader, Harold Overmeyer, a prime suspect.

Brennan observes the hierarchy of the tunnels and suggests that Booth treat Harold with a measure of respect befitting his position in the underground populace. Booth comes to realize that, like himself, Overmeyer is a veteran who has seen and done horrible things in the course of war. Booth turns Harold over to Angela in an attempt to get her to connect with the man, and he ultimately provides a useful clue to the location of the vault and solution of the murder.

As 'The Woman in the Tunnel' opens, Booth, Brennan and Zack are mid-scene, rappelling down the airshaft in the bowels of Washington, D.C. Of course, they weren't really underground. They were on a set built on one of the production's soundstages. But it was still a memorable – and mostly enjoyable – experience for the actors. Eric Millegan's face lights up when he remembers the

Brennan: Can I just have a gun at least until they get here?

Booth: Here (hands her a gun). It's not for shooting rats. It's for psychos with climbing axes.

scene. "Oh my God, it was amazing. It was twenty-feet high or even higher than that and we were pulled up on these harnesses, which really hurt. You didn't realize how much they hurt until they let you down, and then you're like 'Aww! Oh my God!' But that was fun."

Once they are down in the tunnel we see another example of the different ways Booth and Brennan approach a problem. They discover that their evidence is quickly being eaten away by rats dining on the victim. Brennan has an easy solution to the problem. "That was the time that Booth didn't want to give his gun up," explains technical advisor Mike Grasso. "It was kind of funny because they'd been arguing about how she wants a gun and he wouldn't do the paperwork for her. But he's trying to be all nice to her and since she just wants to borrow the gun for a second he hands it over. And then she shoots at the rats! It was funny because poor David asked me, 'What would happen in reality?' And I said, 'The first thing you would do is ask for the day off and then you'd make believe you were never there. You would say, 'I wasn't there at the time. It wasn't my gun!'"

What we try to show with Booth is the fact that although he works outside the box, he still has to deal with a box. And Brennan just doesn't understand that box, not at all. So little moments like that, where he says, 'Do you have any idea the amount of paperwork I'm going to have to do now?' And she replies, 'Why? I just shot the rats.' Those moments sum up the whole gist of their relationship."

Tibia: The inner and larger of the two bones in the lower leg. It extends from the knee to the ankle bone.

Fibula: The outer and narrower of the two bones in the lower leg that runs alongside the tibia.

'Pride' by Syntax, *Meccano Mind*

THE SKULL IN THE DESERT

WRITTEN BY JEFF RAKE DIRECTED BY DONNA DEITCH

GUEST STARRING: JAMES PARKS (SHERIFF DAWES), CLAYTON ROHNER (WAYNE KELLOGG), BRENT BRISCOE (LARRY STANSFIELD), MERCEDES COLON (PROFESSOR INEZ), KALANI QUEYPO (ALEX JOSEPH)

- Angela asks for Brennan's help to identify a skull found while visiting her now missing boyfriend, Kirk. She fears it may be his. Preliminary examination reveals that the age and gender match Kirk's.
- DNA results confirm that the skull is Kirk's. Tests on the hair uncover high levels of **lophophora williamsii**-derived mescaline.
- Small bevel marks where the base of the skull detached from the spinal cord signify para-mortem contact gunshot. Markings on the skull indicate that several desert creatures chewed on it, including a fully-grown coyote with a malformed jaw.
- Naturalist Dr. Inez tracks a GPS collar in the coyote's pack to a remote spot in the desert where the rest of the remains are found. Damage to the remains signifies that the body was dropped from a height, such as from a plane, after death.
- Film from a camera found with the remains has a shot of an unusual outcropping that leads Brennan, Booth, Angela, and the local sheriff to a distant point in the desert where they find the original crime scene. A blood trail shows the victim was dragged to a vehicle and taken away. **Luminol** tests on suspect Wayne Kellogg's vehicle highlight a blood pattern of the victim's body.

Every year for three weeks, Angela has a boyfriend and a vacation in the desert. This year, that time is horribly marred when her boyfriend, Kirk, goes missing at the same time as a human skull arrives on the local sheriff's doorstep. Brennan rushes to her friend's aid, but meets resistance from the local sheriff. A call to Booth brings him out on the case. He arranges for the skull to be sent to the medico-legal lab at the Jeffersonian where it is confirmed to be Kirk's. The investigation switches to recovering the rest of the body and locating his missing guide, and the Sheriff's sister, Dhani.

Angela mourns the loss of a man who loved her, but who she feared she could not fully love in return. She worries that she closed herself off to love since it was her decision to only be together three weeks out of the year. She is, however, able to open herself up enough to hear the desert speak to her and help locate the missing woman.

At the Jeffersonian, Zack is having problems asserting himself while Dr. Brennan is away. Though it seems his co-workers are being unnecessarily harsh toward him, it turns out that Hodgins and Goodman set up the situation in the hope that it would spur Zack on to mature, as it is long past time for him to finish his thesis.

'The Skull in the Desert' is truly a focal episode for Angela's character. Though she's always been seen as the most emotional member of the team, it's here that the audience learns that she has also put up walls to protect her vulnerable side. Angela has mentioned in the course of the series that she has been hurt in the past and, though viewers have yet to find out what specifically affected her, they definitely see the consequences during this episode.

Angela: Three weeks a year. I mean fifteen weeks in total. You think that's crazy.

Brennan: No. It's not typical, that's for sure. And if he was yours, one hundred percent yours for three weeks a year, that's... that's more than I've ever had.

Not surprisingly, this is one of Michaela Conlin's favorite installments, as she relished the discoveries she made about her character. "It was so wonderful to shoot," she notes. "The line when she says, 'I don't think I have a generous heart. I was the one who could only handle three weeks a year.' I used to be really attracted to Angela's strength; now I'm sort of attracted to the other side, the weakness. I think it's more interesting. She is really strong and really bawdy, but I often find in life that those characteristics have a flipside. It's nice that Hart really lets her be a lot of different things."

This episode also provides what is arguably the first glimmer of the developing relationship between Angela and Hodgins. In the opening scene, Hodgins is going over the vacation pictures Angela has sent back from the desert. His behavior borders on jealousy with his sarcastic comments on the vacation spot and a shot of her in a bikini. These feelings will slowly build over the rest of season one and into the second season, finally leading to their engagement.

Lophophora williamsii: Peyote. A catcus native, with small rounded nodules containing mescaline, a hallucinogenic drug sometimes used in Native American rituals.

Luminol: A chemical used to detect trace amounts of blood. When luminol is applied to an area with blood, the resulting chemical reaction will cause the blood to glow.

'Rain' by Patty Griffin, A Kiss in Time
'Too Easy' by One Republic

Insect Activity & Soil Analysis

Dr. Jack Hodgins proudly refers to himself as the Jeffersonian's "bug and slime guy", which is an accurate, if informal, description of his job responsibilities. Insect activity and soil analysis can provide a number of clues to a subject's identity or the events surrounding a victim's death.

Insects

Insects are a natural part of the process of decomposition. Tracing the development of pupal casings and insect life cycles can provide a reliable estimate of the time-frame in which the body has been deceased. For instance, three larval stages of trichoptera and chironomidae found in pond silt beside a body, indicated that the victim had been in that pond for a year and a half ('Pilot').

Examination of insects that have fed off a victim can also provide important clues. When organs may no longer be present, beyond what has been ingested by the insects, those very bugs may be able to reveal what kind of drugs or chemicals were in the victim's body at the time of death.

In the lab, insects can be used as a cleaning agent. Dermestes maculatus are quite thorough at cleaning off any remaining flesh from the bone to allow for a more in-depth skeletal examination ('The Man in the SUV'). The bugs also provide diversionary activities when used in races on a particularly slow evening, though that practice is generally frowned upon by Jeffersonian administrators!

Soil

A natural counterpart to insect activity would be the soil that those bugs can often be found in. As Dr. Hodgins is quick to point out in the lab, the term "dirt" has no meaning. Soil properties differ based on composition, region, environment, and a multitude of other factors that make simple "dirt" useful evidence in a crime. Like their insect counterparts, flora can also aid in determining timeframe. For instance, algae found growing on a body recovered from a bay indicated that it had been submerged for six years ('Two Bodies in the Lab').

First and foremost, soil classification can be used to determine the location of a crime. Silt and pollen found within the skull fractures of the victim of a death row inmate were integral in locating the original crime scene where the victim was murdered ('The Man on Death Row'). The pollen was from spartina alterniflora (smooth cordgrass), which is only found along the Chesapeake Bay, while the silt contained chemicals indicating that it came from an area near a chemical plant. These two factors led investigators to the murder weapon… and two more victims.

In a more personal case for the Jeffersonian staffers, when Doctors Brennan and Hodgins fell victim to the serial killer known as the Gravedigger, they found themselves buried in a subsoil accumulation of agglutinate aridosols, with a limited air supply (the season two episode 'Aliens in a Spaceship'). Thanks to Hodgins' familiarity with soil properties, they were able to send a message back to their co-workers listing the chemical properties of the coal-rich soil in which they were buried. This led Booth and his team to their location and ultimately saved their lives.

THE MAN WITH THE BONE

WRITTEN BY CRAIG SILVERSTEIN
DIRECTED BY JESÚS SALVADOR TREVIÑO

GUEST STARRING: ROBERT FOXWORTH (BRANSON ROSE), RODNEY ROWLAND (DANE MCGINNIS), DAVID WELLS (HARLEY FRANKEL), CULLEN DOUGLAS (HARRY TEPPER), FREDRIC LANE (GILES HARDEWICKE), CHRIS PAYNE GILBERT (ERIC HUGHES), MICHAEL CHIEFFO (MAYOR FRANK NEY), JOHN M. JACKSON (FBI DEPUTY DIRECTOR SAM CULLEN)

When the body of a man is found holding a bone that dates back over 300 years, at a place rumored to have buried pirate treasure, the case takes on a more romanticized air than usual. An examination of the shaft where the man died reveals the rest of the skeleton of what is conjectured to be a pirate – which would support the theory that the dig team is on the path to buried treasure.

During the course of the investigation, the 300 year-old bones – save the finger – are stolen from the lab. It's later determined that the bones had originally been property of the Jeffersonian anyway. The bones were stolen and placed in the shaft as a fake clue that the dig team was on the right track to finding the gold. Dr. Goodman's internal investigation reveals that a security guard had been paid first by the victim and later by his surviving partner to commit the thefts of the bones from both the museum and the medico-legal unit.

A second murder scene leads Booth and Brennan to suspect that the killer was one of the employees on the dig. When they approach Dane McGinnis, he is working with Hodgins, who is diving in the shaft. McGinnis allows Hodgins to resurface safely after he finds a gold coin that may be part of a larger treasure.

"I love it when Jack gets to hang up his turquoise lab coat and see the sun," says TJ Thyne. However, he goes on to admit that his favorite aspects of his character are less action-oriented. Thyne is in fact most interested in Hodgins' emotional journey. "It truly is my favorite part of getting to be him, seeing him deal with relationship issues and real life

Booth: Guy was a Navy Seal.

Brennan: So? You were a guide.

Booth: A Ranger. I was a Ranger, Bones. Okay? I was not a guide. Guides, they show you waterfalls, they sell you cookies. I was a Ranger.

- The body of treasure seeker Ted Macy was found in an underwater shaft. The local coroner wrote it off as an accidental drowning, but a later FBI autopsy revealed a crushed larynx, making it a murder.
- The body was clutching a **phalanx** of unknown origin, causing Special Agent Booth to bring Brennan in on the case. **Radiocarbon dating** determines that the bone is over 300 years old.
- Soil and water are collected from the victim's throat. In order to locate where in the shaft the victim died, Hodgins dives into the dig site to collect soil samples from the top and bottom of the shaft. While submerged, Hodgins locates the complete skeleton with the missing phalanx. His silt samples confirm the victim was killed at the top of the shaft.
- Further examination of the original victim by Jeffersonian staff finds the C-2 through C-4 vertebrae are fractured. The fractures are all left-to-right at approximately forty-five degree angles on each bone, meaning the head was jerked to the left and up, ensuring that the spinal cord would tear. The larynx was crushed when the victim's neck was broken. This is noted to be a special-forces move, indicating that the murderer was in the service, which tracks with the history of an employee on the dig.

character dilemmas," he confirms. "That's what intrigues me most, both as an actor and as an audience member."

Future episodes where Hodgins gets out of the lab may resonate on a more deeply personal level for the character, but there's nothing like the pirate fun he gets to experience in this episode. But Thyne wasn't the only one to enjoy 'The Man with the Bone'. Technical consultant Donna Cline, who is also the storyboard artist behind Angela's drawings, lists the sketch of Hodgins as the pirate as one of her favorite creations for the show. "Everybody remembers that one," she notes. "That was really fun to do."

As this episode proves again, *Bones* is a series that likes to get away from the soundstage. Much of the action in 'The Man with the Bone' supposedly takes place at a federal seaside preserve on Assateague Island; in reality the production never left Los Angeles County.

The show travels beyond the walls of Fox studios often enough for location to be not one, but two full-time jobs. "I have two sets of location managers," explains producer Jan DeWitt. "They alternate odd and even episodes." And, sometimes, an episode is so location intensive that they have to join forces.

Phalanx: Finger bone.

Radiocarbon dating: A method of measuring the naturally occurring isotope carbon with mass number fourteen in organic materials to determine the age of the subject.

'Whistles the Wind' by Flogging Molly, *Within a Mile of Home*

THE MAN IN THE MORGUE

WRITTEN BY ELIZABETH BENJAMIN & NOAH HAWLEY
DIRECTED BY JAMES WHITMORE JR.

GUEST STARRING: MICHELLE HURD (DET. ROSE HARDING), SCOTT LAWRENCE (SAM POTTER), PATRICIA BELCHER (CAROLINE GILLIAN), VICTOR TOGUNDE (JAMES EMBRY), JUDD TRICHTER (DR. RYAN HALLOWAY), KEVIN RANKIN (MIKE DOYLE), COLBY DONALDSON (DR. GRAHAM LEGIERE), GIANCARLO ESPOSITO (RICHARD BENOIT)

New Orleans. Nine months after Hurricane Katrina. Dr. Brennan's idea of a vacation is helping to identify dead bodies unearthed by the hurricane. She becomes embroiled in her own mystery when she wakes up covered in blood and with a day missing from her memory. Booth flies down to assist as they look into the last case she had been working on, a John Doe with ties to voodoo ritual. The case calls into question both Booth and Brennan's belief systems as they learn more about the voodoo religion.

When Brennan is arrested for the murder of a co-worker, Booth brings in a friend from the U.S. Attorney's office to defend her, while the case gets more involved in dark voodoo and another body is found. When Booth and Brennan accompany local police to arrest the suspected murderer, they find her impaled on a ritual spike in her father's voodoo shop. Her father had killed her, hoping to revive her with good voodoo once the case was closed.

Like the earlier Christmas episode ('The Man in the Fallout Shelter') this installment provides another opportunity to explore the religious debate between the empiricist – Brennan – and the devout Catholic – Booth. This issue resonates at the core of these two characters and their relationship, something the writers do not take lightly.

"It's a great debate," says executive producer Stephen Nathan. "It's a wonderful discussion. It's exactly what should be happening in this country, but isn't. In

Brennan: They believe in the same saints you do. And prayer. What they call spells; you call miracles. They have priests.

Booth: We don't make zombies.

Brennan: Jesus rose from the dead after three days.

Booth: Jesus is not a zombie!

- While in New Orleans, Dr. Brennan awakes covered in blood, with a hairline stress fracture on her right **distal radius**, a concussion, a slight fever, and a torn earlobe. She cannot remember the events of the previous day.
- During the missing period of time, Dr. Brennan sent the Jeffersonian staff X-rays of a John Doe #361. Anomalies on his spine indicate the victim suffered from **spina bifida**. He once had a shunt from his brain stem down to his heart, but it was removed more than a decade earlier. A crosscheck of this information with **DMORT** reveals the man's identity as Rene Mouton. Damage to the victim's pubic bone is identified as strike marks from the emblem of a 1959 Cadillac Brougham.
- The body of Dr. Graham Legiere is found in what appears to be a voodoo ritualistic killing. Traces of Dr. Brennan's blood are discovered in his home and his blood matches the stains on her clothing.
- Another morgue employee is found dead during the investigation. He was drugged and a spike was driven through his head during or immediately following sexual intercourse.
- The murders are tied to a member of a voodoo cult known as Secte Rouge. The murderer's father owns a 1959 Cadillac Brougham whose emblem matches the strike wounds on Mouton.

that way, it's very, very, very political. And I don't think we realized that at the time. It's having a dialogue rather than having a war. There's no discussion or dialogue in the country now. It's 'You're right and I'm wrong'; or 'I'm right and you're wrong.' But here we have two people discussing it. And they might be arguing, but the discourse does not end, and it doesn't stop them from working together. In a way it deepens it."

Still, the writers knew they were pushing the limit with the debate in this particular episode. Creator/executive producer Hart Hanson remembers, "I was astounded that Standards and Practices let us have the 'Was Jesus a zombie?' conversation. It's just a very funny thing for her to say. They were down in New Orleans and for her to come out with, 'Well, Jesus rose from the dead after three days.' And Booth to reply, 'Jesus is not a zombie! I should not have to tell you that!' But it never came up with Standards and Practices. I think it was – I don't know exactly why – but I think it was because we were respectful of it."

"It was because it was a discussion," Nathan adds. "Standards and Practices is kind of interesting. They will let us get away with talking about things such as sexual ideals as long as it's from the characters' points of view. As long is it's not just for a cheap laugh."

"Which we are not above," Hanson quickly interjects.

"If we can sneak the cheap laugh in, God knows we will!" Nathan agrees, laughing. "But we have to make it seem like it isn't obvious."

Distal radius: The end of the bone of the forearm, where the wrist joint lies.
Spina bifida: A developmental birth defect resulting in an incompletely formed spinal cord.
DMORT: The Disaster Mortuary Operational Response Team is a collection of experts in the fields of victim identification and mortuary services.

'Tipitina' by Bo Dollis & The Wild Magnolias, *Life is a Carnival*
'No Scratch Blues' by Zydeco All Stars, *The Best of Zydeco Instrumentals*
'Tee Nah Nah' by Buckwheat Zydeco, *Waitin' For My Ya Ya*

THE GRAFT IN THE GIRL

WRITTEN BY GREG BALL & LAURA WOLNER
DIRECTED BY SANFORD BOOKSTAVER

GUEST STARRING: MARK HARELIK (DR. PETER OGDEN), MATT WINSTON (NICK MARTIN), ALEXANDRA KROSNEY (AMY CULLEN), KATIE MITCHELL (MADDIE HASTINGS), PAUL KEELEY (DR. KEN RALSTON), SUMALEE MONTANO (ALEXANDRA COMBS), JOHN M. JACKSON (FBI DEPUTY DIRECTOR SAM CULLEN)

- FBI Deputy Director Cullen's daughter Amy was diagnosed with **Mesothelioma** after receiving a bone graft a year earlier. Amy's X-rays uncover the fact that the bone she received was riddled with osteoporosis, suggesting that the donor was considerably older than the file indicates. A transiliac crest core bone biopsy is performed on Amy confirming that the bone graft was the source of the cancer.
- The case falls under FBI jurisdiction when it is determined that other recipients across state lines have received parts from the diseased donor.
- By scanning the X-rays of all of the graft recipients and pieces from exhumed bodies, the Jeffersonian staff reconstruct the skeleton to reveal the appearance of the original donor. **LIBS** shows that strontium isotope levels suggest he lived on the east coast. Extremely low levels of fluoride, but a high level of **CB** in the bones pinpoint the location to West Virginia.
- The diseased bones are tracked back to a funeral home. Particles of bone dust retrieved from the ventilation system confirm the body was harvested there, along with seven others. The mortuary is linked to a transplant assistant at the hospital where Amy was a patient. The assistant is arrested for performing the illegal harvesting.

When Brennan and Angela meet Deputy Director Cullen's daughter, they are immediately taken with her, both as an interesting medical case and a developing artist respectively. Once it's determined that Amy was poisoned by a diseased bone graft, Brennan and Booth go in search of the company that provided the donation and find that it doesn't exist. The team works to identify how many people may be infected from the same illegal donor and sets up a testing facility at a local hospital. Though the cancer has spread too far in Amy's body to save her, the investigation is able to help many others who are infected. To help Amy make the best of her remaining days, Angela creates a 3-D tour of the Louvre in Paris so she can experience one of the many things on her list of things to do before she dies.

The quote below cuts to the heart of the relationship between Booth and the squints. Booth is dealing with a level of intellect and social awkwardness that he simply doesn't understand or relate to. David Boreanaz is as blunt about Booth's interactions with the squints as his character is with the squints themselves. "I just don't deal with them," he says, speaking for Booth. "I don't have a relationship with them. I honestly try to keep them distant from me – getting information and moving on. If I have to get into Zack's face I will."

Not that the actors playing the squints don't understand the dynamic. Eric Millegan fully comprehends the eccentricities of his character. "I always say I'm not as

Zack: ...I never understood that saying "When your number's up". Numbers and equations are quantitative and predictable. Everyone knows when a number's up.

Booth: How do you listen to this all day?

Brennan: I find intelligence soothing.

smart as Zack and I'm not as stupid as Zack," he explains. "In terms of what he knows as a forensic anthropologist, I don't know any of that stuff, but I'm learning. And there are social things he doesn't understand that I, of course, do! But I think sometimes I'm socially awkward too, in real life. Everybody is."

Though Zack may be intimidated by Booth, Angela seems to get her kicks by playfully flirting with him – and doing all that she can to force him and Brennan together. Angela tends to be his "go to" person when he needs someone who can empathize with a family member or get a read on a suspect. Nonetheless, she will always be a squint in his eyes, as he's quick to point out in 'A Boy in a Bush' when she works some technological magic in front of him and he comments that she's "actually one of them".

With the exception of the second season episode 'The Man in the Mansion' Hodgins is the squint who is least affected by Booth's impression of him. TJ Thyne particularly enjoys the relationship. "It always makes me laugh watching footage of Booth and Jack," he says. "Because Booth is so flippant with Jack and Jack just doesn't care. Booth will say, 'Move on. Stop Hodgins.' And Jack hears him but just ignores him. They annoy each other, but in a harmless yet fun-to-watch way. Fun, lots of fun to play."

Mesothelioma: A type of cancer that forms in the lining that covers much of the body's internal organs. It is often found on the lungs and is linked to exposure to asbestos.

LIBS: Laser Induced Breakdown Spectroscopy provides an elemental analysis of the deceased.

C8: A key ingredient in teflon.

'See the Sun' by Pete Murray, *See The Sun*

'The Dumbing Down of Love' by Frou Frou, *Details*

'Born' by Over the Rhine, *Drunkard's Prayer*

THE SOLDIER ON THE GRAVE

WRITTEN BY STEPHEN NATHAN **DIRECTED BY** JONATHAN PONTELL

GUEST STARRING: ALDIS HODGE (JIMMY MERTON), MATT BATTAGLIA (CAPTAIN WILLIAM FULLER), KIRK B.R. WOLLER (PETER LEFFERTS), MITCH LONGLEY (HANK LUTRELL), STACY HOGUE (PRIVATE JODY CAMPBELL), MONNAE MICHAELL (MRS. MARSHALL)

- A burned body found on the grave of war hero Charlie Kent is believed to be a protester, until he is identified as fellow National Guardsman Devon Marshall.
- Damage to the **external auditory meatus** and scrapings within the cranium indicate that someone jammed an object through Marshall's skull to kill him.
- The investigation reveals sloppy and incomplete records from the attack in Mosul in which Charlie Kent died. Questions about the hero's death force Brennan to request the exhumation of the body.
- The bullets in Kent's body reveal that he died from friendly fire. Crime scene photos suggest that the incident was staged after Kent accidentally fired on an innocent family and another Guardsman shot Kent during the mélèe, making the shooter a suspect in the Marshall murder.
- The Guardsman commits suicide before he can be questioned, but it is later revealed that he was out of town at the time of Marshall's death.
- A dimple on the base of Marshall's skull and discoloration on the vertebrae caused by **pethidine** residue signify that someone jabbed a syringe into his neck to render him immobile. A nine-inch surgical curette is determined to be the murder weapon. The evidence points to the one member of the guard troop with access to medical equipment, Private Jody Campbell.

Tensions run high as Booth and Brennan investigate a death that initially appears to be a war protest. A former soldier himself, Booth is moved by the case to the point that Brennan believes it is affecting his objectivity. Hodgins exacerbates the situation with his anti-government rants, until Angela puts him in his place. The criticism is especially hard on the conspiracy theorist because it comes from Angela.

The murdered man found atop a soldier's grave opens up old wounds for Booth, as he examines the events surrounding a reported insurgent attack in Mosul a year earlier, and forces him to question his own past actions while in uniform. Interviews with the National Guard troops involved in the Mosul incident reveal that they were involved in a cover-up. The man killed and burned atop the grave was dead because a young Private was afraid he was going to come forward and reveal the truth.

Bones functions on many levels. From procedural drama to romantic comedy, the show is often at its most intense when it addresses real-world issues. The producers work diligently to ensure that they examine all sides of a subject, but they can't please everyone. "We got yelled at for being both anti-Iraq and pro-Iraq," reveals Hart Hanson. "When in fact, we were pretty much just 'War is not good.' It was odd. We were really careful not to be political with it."

The phrase "ripped from the headlines" is used a lot with certain television series. And the *Bones* writers have certainly addressed real-world storylines in their own unique way. But there have been several incidences in the course of the show where the episodes predated the

Brennan: ...I can say anything to you without thinking about it first.

Angela: Yeah. Men aren't like us. They're much more fragile and needy. The fact that they think we're the needy ones is a testament to our superiority.

headlines and life imitated art, instead of the other way around. The wartime cover up in this episode had its own real-world counterpart when, in early 2006, U.S. Marines were implicated in the deaths of two-dozen Iraqis. Though the specifics were different, the parallels to this episode were uncanny. "I wrote that episode and it was fiction," Stephen Nathan notes. "A month later, the whole Haditha scandal came out. The episode was not based on that at all. We had no knowledge of it."

But that was not the last time the writers would predict the future. Hanson recalls the same thing happening with the second season episode 'The Boneless Bride in the River'. "We had a story where someone was killed to provide a bride in the afterlife," he explains. "And then they arrested three people in China for doing that: killing people for their bones. Not just grave robbing."

Nathan reminds Hanson of another incident that was imitated in life: "The other one this season of cutting the baby out of the mother," he adds, referring to the episode 'Mother and Child in the Bay'.

Hanson jumps in with, "How about the astronaut? We had a loony toons astronaut story and, in fact, we weren't allowed to use the phrase NASA in it because they said it would never happen ['Spaceman in a Crater']. Next thing you know there's a somewhat similar news story sweeping across the world's media!"

External auditory meatus: The opening in the skull where the auditory nerves feed into the brain, better known as the ear canal.

Pethidine: An opiate/painkiller commonly known as demerol.

THE WOMAN IN LIMBO

WRITTEN BY HART HANSON DIRECTED BY JESÚS SALVADOR TREVIÑO

GUEST STARRING: LOREN DEAN (RUSS BRENNAN), PAT SKIPPER (VINCE MCVICAR), COBY RYAN MCLAUGHLIN (DAVID SIMMONS), DEE WALLACE STONE (SPECIAL AGENT CALLIE WARNER)

In September 1998 the bones of an unidentified woman were sent to the Jeffersonian where they remained in bone storage until Zack had the time to attempt identification. The bones proved to belong to Christine Brennan, Dr. Brennan's missing mother.

Brennan struggles to reconnect with her brother, Russ, whom she feels abandoned her following their parents' disappearance. Their reunion continues to be marred as it is revealed that their parents changed their identities when Temperance was two. Russ reveals that her real name was Joy.

Brennan's parents were on a list of federal offenders as part of a group of armed robbers. The agent in charge of the original investigation claims that Brennan's parents never belonged in that crew because they were never violent, and only stole from safe deposit boxes. A job in 1978 went bad and innocent bystanders were either killed or injured. Two years later, one of the crew, McVicar, turned state's evidence and sent the rest to jail.

Booth believes that McVicar found the Brennans years later, forcing Temperance's parents to flee to keep their children safe. McVicar eventually caught up with them, injuring Christine Brennan in a manner that proved fatal. The case ends with Tempe and Russ reunited, but wondering if their father may still be alive. That question is answered when they return home to a message waiting on Temperance's answering machine...

The story of Brennan's missing parents was first introduced in the pilot, while several episodes touched on her

Man's Voice: Temperance, you have to stop looking. You have to stop looking for me right now. This is bigger and worse than you know. Please stop now.

Booth: Who's that?

Man's Voice: Stop.

Brennan: That was my father.

- When Zack finalizes the tissue markers on the skull of a Jane Doe from bone storage, Angela gives the woman a face on the Angelator. Upon seeing it, Brennan insists that he did something wrong and demands to see the artifact bag that accompanied the body. Inside it is a dolphin belt buckle that belonged to her mother. Further tests confirm her identity.
- Residue in the accompanying soil indicates the body was buried for at least five years before it was discovered and brought to the Jeffersonian in 1998, which places the death two years after Brennan's parents went missing.
- Cause of death was a subdural hematoma, though there does not appear to be a wound on the outer skull. At 500 times magnification, microscopic fractures are found on the **osteons** suggesting that a smaller wound grew over the course of a year and eventually proved fatal. The pattern suggests a blow from the front that grazed the skull as the victim was pulled away at the last moment.
- Angela works with Brennan's brother, Russ, to reconstruct the face of a man he saw back when he was seven. The image matches that of Vince McVicar, a former associate of their parents, currently under witness protection. A farm instrument found in McVicar's barn matches the wound pattern on the victim's skull.

childhood and how their disappearance affected her. 'The Woman in Limbo' is the first time the show really deals with the mystery of the disappearance. "Originally, Brennan's back-story was supposed to unfold slowly over the course of season one," Hart Hanson reveals. "I had it all figured out. I had it *all* figured out. But we are an episodic show and the desire of both the network and the studio – and it's a good desire – is for us to remain episodic. So that people can come in at any time."

With serialized shows like *24* and *Prison Break* on the schedule, Fox was looking for a self-contained show where the audience didn't have the pressure of missing an episode meaning that they'd be missing an important part of the puzzle.

Revising his original plan for Brennan's back-story did present its fair share of problems for Hanson. "We had the situation of trying to get out that entire back-story in one episode," he explains. "Another thing we wrestled with is parceling out these bits of information in a way where the audience doesn't need a man with a hat to come and point to a diagram. If I'd known [this is how we'd end up doing it] I would have made it a much simpler back-story. But it has worked out well, because it's rich."

Stephen Nathan agrees, "It's such a wonderful position to put her in," he adds. "She solves crimes and is looking for great order in the universe – while, in fact, her life is the most chaotic of all."

Osteon: A central canal occurring in compact bone.

'New Girl Now' by Honeymoon Suite, *Honeymoon Suite*
'As the Stars Fall Away' by Peter Himmelman, *Unstoppable Forces*

THE KNEE BONE'S CONNECTED TO THE...

THE GENESIS OF SEASON TWO

The transition to a second season of any series often brings changes in front of and behind the cameras as the producers learn from their first year and approach the second with an eye to continuing for many years to come. The second season of *Bones* would see new faces in key roles onscreen and off as it settled into the new season. The change most noticeable to the audience would be the loss of Dr. Daniel Goodman, as portrayed by Jonathan Adams.

"He was a wonderful, wonderful actor," writer/ executive producer Stephen Nathan notes. "We loved Jonathan. But there was no real function for him in the show. Servicing his character always took us out of the stories. We tried many things through the year and everything we gave him, he made it work beautifully."

"We needed someone closer to where the rubber hits the road," creator/executive producer Hart Hanson continues. "Someone who was not an administrator, but who was working on the case as well."

Cam: What if I fire her? What would you do?

Booth: I'm with Bones, Cam. All the way. Don't doubt it for a second.

Considering one of the initial edicts from the studio was that they did not want to focus solely on the "dry brittle bones" every week, the executive producers decided they needed a character that would give them more access to what they call the "squishy bits". As such, they cast Tamara Taylor as Dr. Camille Saroyan, the new head of forensics with an interesting link to Booth's past. "There are more opportunities to do more gross stuff with Cam," Nathan explains. "All the flesh – the bits of science that we wouldn't see from the other squints. She opened up the cases by being both a pathologist and coroner." Though initially Taylor was only brought on to appear in six episodes, the character became so important to the story, and the actress to the cast, that she was asked to stay and became a regular castmember. But she wasn't the only new face at the start of the second season.

The producers were also concerned about the look of *Bones*. In the first season, they had two different directors of photography as they worked to develop the visual style of the series. Coming into the second season they wanted someone on staff who could be the "set guy" to keep control over the visual aspect of production, while Hanson and Nathan focused predominantly – though not exclusively – on the writing – the real bones of *Bones*. Enter Tony Wharmby, a freelance director/producer who worked on *The X-Files* and had already directed the first season episode 'The Man on the Fairway'.

Wharmby describes his unusual role on the set and what he feels he brings to the production: "I'm very much a producer who is concerned with what I call 'visual identity'," he explains. "I don't like television shows to look like other television shows or even television shows at all. My brief was to give the show that quality of visual identity."

One of Wharmby's first actions in his new role was the hiring of experienced director of photography Gordon Lonsdale to help bring his vision for the show to the

Below: David Boreanaz and David Duchovny on the set of the episode 'Judas on a Pole', which Duchovny directed.

screen. "Gordon and I worked for about five or six weeks at the beginning of the season," Wharmby reveals. "Working out the show, walking the sets, making changes to the sets. Just really swapping ideas about how we felt the show should look, and ideas for how he would change the lighting to make the show look the way I thought it should look, and so on."

Wharmby came in not only to produce the visuals, but also to direct the actors. "The second part of my brief was that I watched very carefully the performances of the cast, and the relationships and how they gelled," he notes. "However glamorous and gorgeous the show looks, when it comes down to it what the audience watches are the performances and relationships."

Gordon Lonsdale is enthusiastic about the challenges and satisfactions presented by working on a series with as many emotional nuances as *Bones*. "Every *Bones* episode is not exactly the same," he explains. "So as I read through a new script, and as the pictures of the locations come in, I get a feeling for what I can do, and which scenes are going to be dark and which are going to be bright. I look out for the humorous scenes because I don't play those quite as dark as some others. I'm looking at what can I do with my

Brennan: I miss organic chemistry class. Those were good times.

Zack: I miss my first microscope.

Booth: I miss normal people.

lighting to help tell the story and support it. If it goes dark, then my lighting is going to go dark. If it's humorous then it won't be as dark because I want to support the emotions and things that are happening in the script."

The core concept of the show remained the same for season two: using forensic science to solve the most hideous crimes, while skillfully weaving comedy and romance into the mix. Another important element that carried over from the first season was the show's ability to comment on real world issues, whether they came up by coincidence or by plan.

"We're not doing a ripped from the headlines show," executive producer Barry Josephson is quick to point out. "However, we are doing a show that is socially, morally and worldly relevant. I think if you don't do that then the audience will change the channel because they're just not intrigued. I think the great thing that Hart Hanson and Stephen Nathan have done is that when they break a story they choose issues that they've talked about or argued about themselves. Or occasionally, there's just something so compelling in the news or in the world that you can't avoid it. But I think for the most part they've been very clever, along with the writing staff, at breaking great stories and keeping the show very contemporary and fresh."

In approaching the second season, Hanson and Nathan took cues from their first year in keeping the story evolving in a serialized way, while still producing self-contained episodes. The season opens with Brennan returning from a vacation with her formerly estranged brother, and her first encounter her new boss, Dr. Camille Saroyan. The relationships will grow and change over the course of the season as the characters settle into the storylines that had been established in year one. They will continue to solve gruesome and intricate cases while negotiating their often-complex personal lives. Brennan will meet her long-lost father; Booth will start seeing a therapist; Angela and Hodgins will fall in love – and, perhaps most surprisingly of all, Zack will get a haircut!

ACCESS PASS
NAME: TEMPERANCE BRENNAN
PASS CODE: 17573220

SEASON TWO

Regular cast:

David Boreanaz: *Special Agent Seeley Booth*

Emily Deschanel: *Dr. Temperance Brennan*

Michaela Conlin: *Angela Montenegro*

Eric Millegan: *Dr. Zack Addy*

TJ Thyne: *Dr. Jack Hodgins*

Tamara Taylor: *Dr. Camille Saroyan*

THE TITAN ON THE TRACKS

WRITTEN BY **HART HANSON** *DIRECTED BY* **TONY WHARMBY**

GUEST STARRING: CHRISTINE ESTABROOK (LISA SUPAC), RAY WISE (RICK TURCO), ANN CUSACK (LAWYER), TIMOTHY LANDFIELD (DANIEL BURROWS), SAM WITWER (MITCHELL DOWNS), ALEX HYDE-WHITE (MR. HOBBES), ALLISON DUNBAR (BRIANNA LYNCH), JONELL KENNEDY (DR. LAWRENCE)

After vacationing with her brother, Brennan tells Booth that she wants to find their father. They are sidetracked by a more pressing case when a train carrying the now deceased Senator Paula Davis crashes into a car. At the crime scene, Booth introduces Brennan to Dr. Camille Saroyan, the new head of forensics at the Jeffersonian's medico-legal unit, and Brennan's new boss.

It is determined that the car driver – a businessman under investigation by the SEC (Securities and Exchange Commission) named Warren Lynch – was dead long before the train struck, suggesting that the train crash was not an accident. Lynch and his personal investigator, Rick Turco, conspired to make the businessman disappear for a few days in order to cash in on the stock when it plummeted following the report of his death. When things got too hot, Turco is suspected of killing Lynch for real. Booth and Brennan trick Turco into admitting that he helped stage the first death, but nothing more.

Meanwhile, the man charged with the murder of Brennan's mother is killed while in a federal holding facility. An interview with the murderer suggests that Brennan's father arranged the hit. When she visits her mother's grave Brennan finds a small silver dolphin had been left there, presumably by her father.

It helps to open the season with a bang – such as a train crash – to hook the viewers and get them back into a show that's been off the air for months. One of the other advantages for this episode is that, being the first show of the season, the production has extra time to come in, plan it and get it just right.

In discussing the train crash, co-executive producer Steve Beers brings up a recurring problem for the production regarding the California vegetation. "Figuring out the train crash

Brennan: ...Come on, Booth. The part of you with the big gambling problem must love this idea.

Booth: Right there. Mm-hm. That's the reason you didn't get Cam's job.

• From dental records and a melted ID bracelet, the male driver of a car that was struck by a train is identified as Warren Lynch of Lynchpin International.

• Accelerants are found after burn damage to the driver's body is determined to be more intense than one would expect for a car fire. Jagged edges to the breaks, small fragments, lack of circular or radiating fractures, or adherent **bone spurs** indicate the body was dead at least six hours before being struck by the train.

• Drugs in the victim's system match that of a shipment local police confirm have killed fourteen users in the past week.

• A facial reconstruction proves that the body did not in fact belong to Warren Lynch. The dental records are revealed to have been expertly faked. An interview with a known drug dealer leads investigators to provide a genuine ID on the victim, a homeless man.

• The real Warren Lynch is found, after having been thrown from a speeding car. He'd been badly beaten and is unconscious, suffering from a severe brain injury. It is unlikely he will wake up.

• A photo from the Maryland State Police traffic cameras shows Lynch in his car hours before the crash. His personal investigator can be seen in a reflection driving beside Lynch, implying he was involved in the murders of both men.

was a lot of fun," he says. "It was originally written as a day scene but we realized that, number one: it wasn't going to be as spectacular as the lights and the sparks and all the commotion of night; and number two: there were palm trees all around. So by shooting at night and only lighting what we wanted to see, we were able to take Southern California out of the train crash, which was shot on these tracks that go through orange groves and a subdivision up in Fillmore. It was remarkable the way it came out."

But palm trees weren't the only problem the production was facing as the new director of photography, Gordon Lonsdale, recalls: "We knew that it got dark around nine p.m. and started getting bright around four a.m., so Tony Wharmby, the director, and I had to lay out everything." Working with the gaffer and key grip, Lonsdale set up two large lights going in each direction. That way, they could shoot in one direction and be lit, then turn off parts of the lights on one end and turn on the lights at the other and they'd be lit for the other side. "We knew we only had a finite amount of time," Lonsdale explains. "But I thought it looked really good, and the program worked. You just have to plan and prepare before you go."

Bone spurs: Bony projections that form along joints.

'The Greatest' by Cat Power, *The Greatest*

'Be Here Now' by Ray LaMontagne, *Till The Sun Turns Black*

MOTHER AND CHILD IN THE BAY

WRITTEN BY STEPHEN NATHAN DIRECTED BY JESÚS SALVADOR TREVI

GUEST STARRING: KATE NORBY (KAREN TYLER), KIRSTEN POTTER (MARY CORBIS), SHANE JOHNSON (KYLE RICHARDSON), BRUCE FRENCH (DENNIS CAMPBELL), CARYN WEST (PATRICIA CAMPBELL), TANGIE AMBROSE (FAITH DAVIS), JESSICA WRIGHT (TINA HOLMES), JESSICA CAPSHAW (REBECCA STINSON)

- The body of a missing pregnant woman washes up on the shore of the Delaware Bay. Multiple stab wounds reveal that it was a violent attack. Her unborn child's remains are found with the body.
- In a practical experiment, the staff takes turns stabbing a body double to determine the equivalent force necessary to cause wounds that would match the victim's. From the depth of the stab wound, the size, weight, and body type of the assailant most closely matches Angela, indicating the attacker was likely female.
- Tissue from the fetus shows evidence of **escitalopram**, which would have been passed through the mother's body, though there was no evidence in her remains. An examination of the baby's skull shows that the bones had shifted and overlapped because the child had passed through the birth canal. The baby was born alive and lived about two weeks, meaning the baby did not belong to the victim.
- Knife marks on the lower ribs are found to have been made by a scalpel used to remove the victim's child.
- The murderer is determined to be one of the women in the victim's baby group, a veterinarian with medical training and equipment that allowed her to remove the baby after her own child had died.

While investigating a high-profile case of a murdered pregnant woman, Booth is also dealing with his ex-girlfriend's new relationship. Her boyfriend is spending more time with their son Parker than Booth would like. He runs a background check on the new beau, which leads to an argument with his ex, Rebecca, in which she reminds him that he has no legal visitation rights as they were never married. Observing the situation, Brennan tries to figure out why anyone would want to get married and have children, seeing the complications they lead to. In the end, Rebecca brings her boyfriend to meet Booth and they have coffee together with Parker.

Along similar lines of building relationships, Doctors Brennan and Saroyan are still trying to develop their working relationship. Their divergent approaches to the case cause some friction between the pair, with Zack caught in the middle.

Usually when a new female character is introduced to a television series, the writers like to create conflict between her and the existing alpha female. Though Cam's introduction to *Bones* may seem to follow that pattern, there is a distinct difference from the usual cattiness one might find on other shows. "They made it more intelligent," explains Tamara Taylor, who plays Cam. "The writers on this show are just so great and when given the option the high road is *always* the one that they take. I was really grateful that it wasn't just a catfight."

The other women on the show agree and add that this fresh approach to female characters in television was one of the main things that attracted each of them to the show. "You can tell the

Zack: There was a dead fish under the plastic.

Hodgins: Ooh, and it's not even my birthday.

way the writers view women," says Michaela Conlin. "Emily and I were just joking that the women in this show have the best offices. Which I really think is a testament to Hart Hanson because he really knows how to write for women. It's a real rarity. It's nice that we're allowed to show up the men. It's really fun."

Emily Deschanel echoes Conlin's comments. "I love the fact that the main male character doesn't understand half the things that we say and we need to educate him. He's just more street smart than he is book smart. The three main female characters all have the best offices and areas to work in, while the male scientists have much smaller offices and areas. Angela has a huge office with her holographic computer, the Angelator; and Cam has the autopsy room with her own office. My office is fantastic and has all these artifacts and art pieces from around the world, as well as skulls and mummies and so on. It just says something when that's the case. I can't think of one other television show where the women are better equipped than the men."

Escitalopram: A drug prescribed for depression.

THE BOY IN THE SHROUD

WRITTEN BY GARY GLASBERG DIRECTED BY SANFORD BOOKSTAVER

GUEST STARRING: LEAH PIPES (KELLY MORRIS), DYLAN MCLAUGHLIN (ALEX MORRIS), PAMALA TYSON (FRAN DUNCAN), JON SKLAROFF (KEVIN DUNCAN), WILLIAM BUMILLER (MR. CRANE), KATHLEEN GATI (MRS. CRANE), TARA KARSIAN (DIANE CHILD), KIM STAUNTON (SUZANNE), SCOTT LEAVENWORTH (CARTER)

- An overturned garbage truck uncovers the decaying remains of a young male with massive contusions congruent with a fall onto a hard surface. Weighted impact against the **scapula** and **clavicle** indicate he was struck prior to the fall, but not hard enough to cause death.
- Fabric covering the face has tissue stains around the eye sockets, the nose and the mouth, essentially providing a photo negative of the victim's features. Using computer **tomography** a facial reconstruction is created and run through the missing persons database, identifying the victim as Dylan Crane, aged seventeen. His girlfriend, a foster child named Kelly Morris, is also missing.
- DNA from the tissue under the victim's fingernails is female. Nail polish is found in gouges on his arm along with rust, which is also in the victim's upper back and shoulder — he was probably struck by a rusty pipe.
- Examination of the garbage surrounding the body suggests it was dumped near a Russian restaurant, leading investigators to the warehouse where the victim died.
- A recreation of the murder implies that someone had struck Dylan with a pipe, forcing him through the window, while Kelly had tried to save him. The accidental murderer is determined to be Kelly's younger brother, Alex.

When a case points to a foster kid as first the victim then possibly the murderer, Cam is quick to make assumptions based on her experience working in law enforcement over the years. A product of the foster system herself, Brennan's defense of the foster children is immediate. Considering the negative perception of such children, she wonders if people think the same of her.

While pursuing the case, Booth and Brennan come across a couple that try to help the street kids. The husband, however, is not quite such a good samaritan – his past charges of pedophilia prove not just to be in the past. His wife kills him and turns herself in.

As the case continues Brennan and Saroyan butt heads over their different approaches to the investigation. Cam is more intuitive and jumps to conclusions, while Brennan is empirical and only deals with the facts. The situation descends to a point where Brennan admits that she cannot work in Saroyan's way, causing Cam to ask if that means she's quitting. Angela quickly comes to her friend's defense, saying that if Brennan leaves, they all leave. Later, Booth confirms that he'd go too and explains to Cam that Brennan was a foster child. Finally, the two women work together to resolve their issues.

When filming on set, the *Bones* crew works in a largely self-contained area. Traveling between two soundstages, they have everything they would need in the trailers and offices on the Fox Studios lot. They can build their sets and pretty much do whatever they want with them, within reason. Going on location, they have to pack up the trucks and the people and function under a different set of rules. One of the people most affected by those rules is set decorator Kim Wannop, but she fully appreciates

Booth: Teenage boys love nothing more than the idea of saving the damsel in distress.

Brennan: How do you know?

Booth: Well, because I was... You know, I was a teenage boy.

what a location provides in return. "Shooting on location gives the show a better sense of reality," she explains. "When dressing a location there are many different factors and restrictions, such as not putting holes in walls when hanging pictures or sconces, and sometimes pieces of furniture cannot get into certain spaces because of small doors or a lack of elevators. There is more freedom on a stage because we can basically hang whatever we want and the space is – if it's a living room – usually bigger than normal. The more challenging locations are usually our gritty sets. From train derailments, overturned trash trucks, homeless encampments to sewage plants, sometimes we get dirty."

Dirty may be a bit of an understatement. Even though much of the death and decay featured on the series is created by makeup wizards, sometimes the yuck factor can be real, as with the garbage seen in this episode. Prop master Ian Scheibel vividly recalls the trials everyone had to endure: "When the scene was first shot the cast and crew were joined by thousands of maggots, flies and beetles... and a few turkey carcasses. A lot of the disgusting close-ups were shot several weeks later – the shots that looked like old meat mixed with Jell-o were, in fact, just that."

Scapula: Either of two triangular bones that form the back of the shoulders, known commonly as the shoulder blades.

Clavicle: A long curved bone connecting the upper breastbone to the shoulder blades. Better known as the collarbone.

Tomography: A technique of using ultrasound or X-rays to produce a focused image of structures within the body.

'Bring on the Wonder' by Susan Enan, featuring Sarah McLachlan

THE BLONDE IN THE GAME

WRITTEN BY NOAH HAWLEY DIRECTED BY BRYAN SPICER

GUEST STARRING: HEATH FREEMAN (HOWARD EPPS), CHRISTIE LYNN SMITH (CAROLINE EPPS), JIM JANSEN (GRANT HATHAWAY), IRENE ROSEEN (SISTER KAREN DUNNE), DOHN NORWOOD (MR. HATHAWAY)

• A man walking his dog finds the remains of a female victim in her late teens. Cause of death was blunt trauma to the back of the skull, with a wound in the shape of a tire iron. Placement of wrists and ankles suggest she was bound before being buried face down. Pupal casings and insect remains indicate she was buried seven to ten years ago. The manner of death and timeframe implies the murderer is incarcerated serial killer Howard Epps.

• A **hamate** bone is found with the body that does not belong to the victim. Minute traces of gypsum and selenium are on the bone, in addition to **phenolphthalein**, which leads Booth and Brennan to the remains of another victim in a mine.

• The second victim is also female, in her mid-teens, with bone damage indicating she was hung upside down. This does not fit the original killer's pattern. Dental work identifies her as Sarah Koskoff, aged sixteen, who disappeared only three weeks earlier, meaning the serial killer has an accomplice. The victim has a school medallion that signifies there is a third victim in play who is possibly still alive.

• Upon determining that the serial killer's accomplice is a postal worker, investigators search an abandoned postal sorting facility where they find the missing girl.

A body is found that appears to be linked to death-row inmate Howard Epps ('The Man on Death Row'), beginning what the serial killer considers a game between him and Brennan. It's effectively a twisted scavenger hunt to find more victims' remains, during which Booth and Brennan meet the killer's new wife, Caroline Epps. When a clue suggests they have to destroy evidence, they find information leading to another victim in a fresh grave, suggesting Epps has an accomplice on the outside.

Booth and Brennan learn that a third victim is possibly still alive and that the accomplice is likely the postal worker who found the first body. When they arrive at the location where they believe the girl is being held, Booth hands Brennan a gun. The suspect manages to get the upper hand on Booth, forcing Brennan to shoot and kill the man to save her partner. Booth then helps Brennan cope with the idea of taking a man's life.

Eyebrows are raised when Angela refers to Hodgins as 'Hodgie' at work. Then later, she helps him calm down sufficently to hypothesize a location on the missing girl, when the girl's life depends on a quick rescue.

After multiple requests for a gun throughout the first season, this case is the first time Booth actually hands Brennan a weapon without any playful banter surrounding it, demonstrating the gravity of the situation. This action effectively saves Booth's life, but also affects Brennan deeply as she is forced to take a life. Preparing for these scenes, the actors relied on their technical advisor, Mike Grasso, for more than just the proper way to hold a gun.

"Emily was a little thrown off by having to kill someone on the show," admits Grasso. "She didn't know how to react to that. I sat her down and explained to her what it really meant to shoot somebody. I also talked about it a lot with David, so

Hodgins: A Freemason symbol? Hey, this explains the buried face down thing. Ah, it's all starting to come together. These crossed hammers prove that Epps is working for the top level of the Illuminati!

Zack: That's the cartographic symbol for a mine.

that at the end of the story, when they're sitting down and he speaks to her, he kind of guides her through the experience. It's good. It shows the mindset of the show. Sometimes things need to be done and people don't understand that, 'Okay, you still took someone's life.' But sometimes, when things need to be done, that's enough. You can work your way through it."

On a lighter note, we again see touches of the burgeoning relationship between Angela and Hodgins. Though their flirtation continues to develop slowly, it is moving at a much faster pace than any potential relationship between the two lead characters. The actors and producers believe that counterbalance between the two couples is necessary for the series. Hart Hanson explains, "We knew that when you build up a certain amount of sexual tension you have to let it off somehow, so the audience doesn't feel constantly on the edge. So you start to look at what other people Brennan and Booth could be with and then at a possible stocking horse relationship. Hodgins and Angela are kind of going through what the audience wants Brennan and Booth to go through."

Hamate: A hook-shaped bone in the wrist.

Phenolphthalein: A chemical that changes color in basic solutions. It can be used as a laxative.

'It Don't Matter to the Sun' by Rosie Thomas, *If Songs Could Be Held*

THE TRUTH IN THE LYE

WRITTEN BY SCOTT WILLIAMS **DIRECTED BY** STEVEN DEPAUL

GUEST STARRING: *MELINDA MCGRAW (GAYLE SEAVER), SUSAN SANTIAGO (LILA TURNER), KERI LYNN PRATT (CHLOE DANIELS), BRUCE NOZICK (PETE VALERA), LAMONT THOMPSON (COP), JESSICA CAPSHAW (REBECCA STINSON)*

- A crime scene at a construction site uncovers the remains of a victim that are almost entirely liquefied from sitting two to three days in a tub full of domestic corrosives.
- Marrow cells exhibit a lack of collagen, which indicates a mild case of **osteogenesis imperfecta**, which would have been passed on to the victim's children. A database of children with the disease is checked for any families where the father is missing. Interviews with two mothers reveal they were both married to the same man. Later the investigation uncovers he impregnated a third woman who works at the construction site.
- A mark on the skull fragment signifies that blunt-force trauma was the cause of death. A second examination of the crime scene finds a junction box with a single brown hair embedded in it.
- The evidence shows the victim died in a fight when his head struck the junction box. The murderer covered it up by shooting him in the head so it looked like a suicide. The victim's wives and girlfriend then covered that up with the chemical solution to make it look like murder.
- When a crown is found in the tub that did not come from the victim's mouth, it is matched to the site foreman, who recently had work done on his teeth, proving him to be the murderer.

Booth makes the "huge mistake" of sleeping with his ex-girlfriend and the mother of his child for the fourth time in the past year. When Rebecca answers Booth's cell-phone call from Brennan afterwards, the scientist hypothesizes on what she had interrupted. Brennan and Booth discuss his personal affairs as they investigate the gruesome case of an almost totally liquefied body in a tub.

Booth's personal business travels quickly through the squints, with Cam the first to comment on it directly, as the two were previously involved. Booth is upset that Brennan was gossiping about his love life, but Brennan claims she was just observing the typical behavior of higher primates. When Brennan runs into Rebecca later she asks why she didn't accept Booth's marriage proposal, suggesting this still bothers him. Using that information, Rebecca is able to help Booth move on... which leads him into bed with Cam.

Executive producers Hart Hanson and Stephen Nathan recount the trouble they got into over this most gruesome episode of *Bones*...

Stephen Nathan: "That was the best Standards and Practices phone call I ever had. Standards and Practices always say, 'Well, can you cut back on the blood here, and this body's a little disgusting.' We're very cooperative with them."

Hart Hanson: "He's underselling. Stephen is brilliant with Standards and Practices. Because all I do is get mad. I just get mad. Stephen... wow."

Stephen Nathan: "We always try to work it out with them. But with that one – which was hilarious – they said, 'Now this is just too disgusting.' And I said, 'Why? I don't understand why it's

Brennan: It's nothing to be ashamed of Booth. Humans act upon a hierarchy of needs, and sex is very highly ranked. It's an anthropological inevitability.

Booth: Thank you Bones. I really appreciate you boiling me down to your anthropological inevitabilities.

Brennan: Sure. Anytime.

disgusting.' They replied, 'Well, it's just... when you look at it, it's just awful.' I responded, 'We've literally had bodies torn apart by dogs, with eyeballs falling out and stuff like that. All you see is the top of a skull and some slime.' And they said, 'I know, but what it makes you think...' So, I said, 'Now look. You're asking me to remove your thoughts. I cannot remove your thoughts with the show. As much as I would like to make you comfortable with this scene, all we're showing is some goo. It's just basically, a bowl of pudding. And what it makes you think is out of my control, so there's nothing I can cut from the show that's going to make you feel better about it."

Hart Hanson: "But the fact is, they were right."

Stephen Nathan: "It was gross!"

Hart Hanson: "It was totally gross... and disgusting. To this day – no doubt everyone agrees – our most revolting thing, and the most fun to add sound to!"

Stephen Nathan: "It's so slurpy and gross."

Hart Hanson: "And what did you do? You removed a bubble."

Stephen Nathan: "I removed two bubbles –"

Hart Hanson: "Blup. Blup."

Stephen Nathan: "– of the gas coming up from the decomposing body."

Hart Hanson: "That's what he agreed to."

Stephen Nathan: "But it was revolting. It was also one of our funniest episodes. We actually found in that episode that the grosser something is, the funnier it can be!"

Osteogenesis imperfecta: Known as brittle bone disease, it is a genetic bone disorder in which the afflicted have either less or a poorer quality of collagen in the bone, resulting in weak or fragile bones.

'Here's to the Heroes' by The Ten Tenors, *Here's to the Heroes*

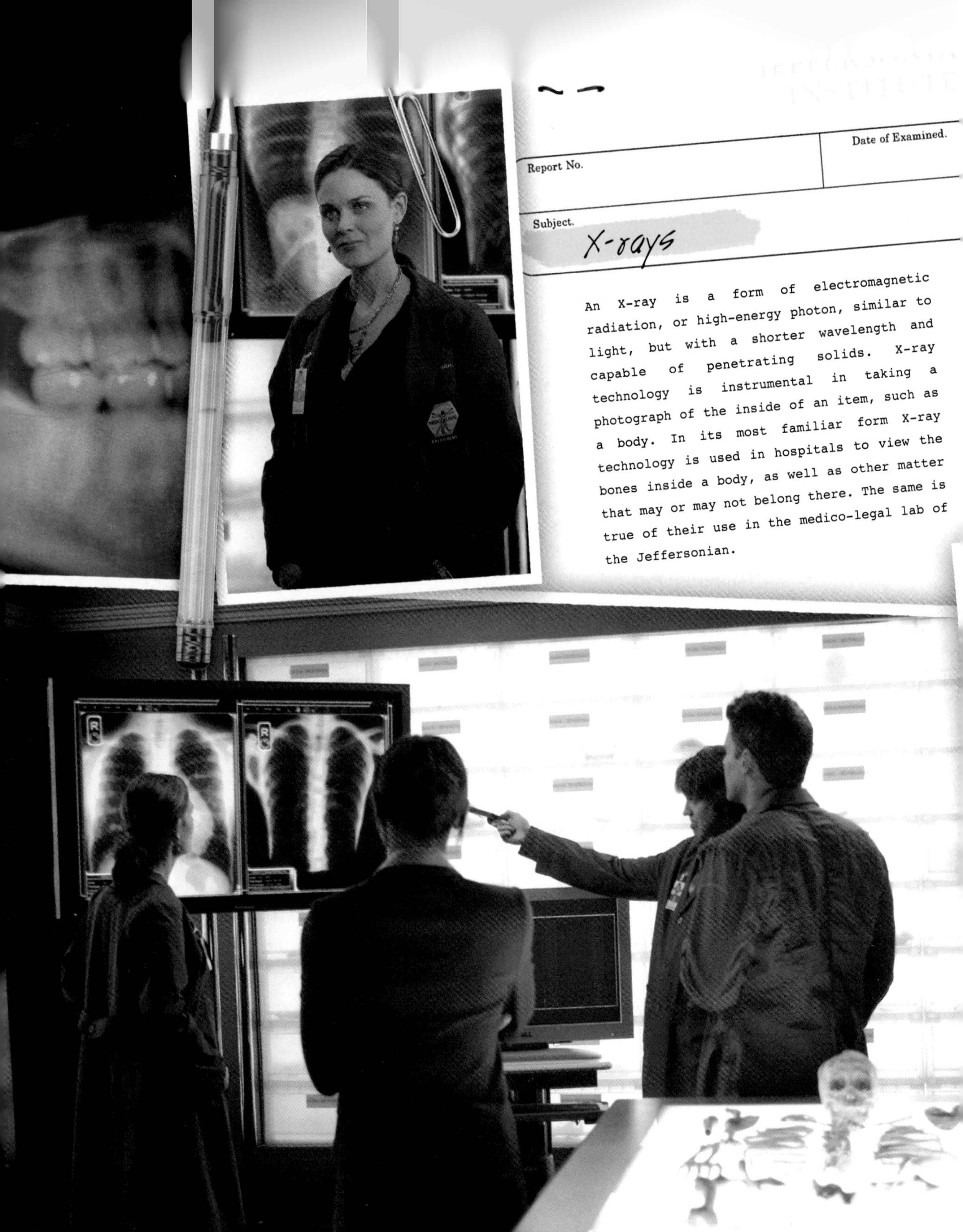

Report No.

Date of Examined.

Subject. X-rays

An X-ray is a form of electromagnetic radiation, or high-energy photon, similar to light, but with a shorter wavelength and capable of penetrating solids. X-ray technology is instrumental in taking a photograph of the inside of an item, such as a body. In its most familiar form X-ray technology is used in hospitals to view the bones inside a body, as well as other matter that may or may not belong there. The same is true of their use in the medico-legal lab of the Jeffersonian.

X-rays as Records

X-ray images are an integral part of the science involved in the forensic study of a corpse. The first stage is a surface exam of the body, followed by recording X-ray images of the corpse before the body is opened for a more direct examination. This is an important process of study because the unexpected can happen during an autopsy, so it is essential to have X-rays to record the original state of the bones and the body should anything go wrong. X-rays can also provide a warning should there be anything specific the coroner would need to be aware of before cutting into the body.

X-rays to Identify

X-rays are particularly useful in identifying foreign masses that may be found within a body. In the interest of time, it may not be expedient to examine every inch of an unknown corpse right away, when an X-ray will often indicate the presence of anything from hip replacements to breast implants that can ultimately be used in assisting with identification.

On a similar note, one of the primary tools used in identifying bodies are dental records, which would contain X-rays of the victim's teeth and jaw. A comparison of the physical skeleton to these records is often useful when fingerprints are not available and DNA tests would take too much time.

X-rays can also be useful in that they can be kept in files long after a body is interred or even cremated. In a case where a body went missing ('The Man in the Morgue') X-rays of the victim provided a much-needed clue that ultimately led to his identification. Marks on the bones in the image also revealed the murder weapon; in this case, the grille of a classic car.

In a rare case, the Jeffersonian staff was able to use a collection of X-rays to piece together the identity of a bone-graft donor who died of cancer ('The Graft in the Girl'). In this investigation, numerous people had been infected with bone grafts that were effectively poisoned with cancer. By taking the infected bone from the exhumed body, in combination with the X-rays from the still-living bone recipients, Jeffersonian researchers were able to connect the grafts and piece together a skeletal framework for the donor to help in determining what the man looked like.

The Limitations of X-Rays

X-Rays are not a perfect science in the lab, however. Frequently a spot on an X-ray can be merely a shadow, or it could be something more. In those cases, a direct examination of the bone is necessary, which cuts to the core of the work done by the forensic anthropologist.

THE GIRL IN SUITE 2103

WRITTEN BY CHRISTOPHER AMBROSE DIRECTED BY KAREN GAVIOLA

GUEST STARRING: DANNY WOODBURN (ALEX RADSWELL), BERTILA DAMAS (JUDGE DOLORES RAMOS), LAURA LEIGH HUGHES (JILL WINOKUR), ANDRES LONDONO (ANTONIO RAMOS), CARLOS LACAMARA (JUAN RAMOS), JOHN KASSIR (LAWRENCE MELVOY), CERINA VINCENT (DENISE)

- An explosion leaves four dead at a cocktail party with a high-ranking Colombian judge in attendance. A fifth body, presumed to be a female bomber, is found in a chandelier.
- Arson investigators determine that the explosion originated in the room next to the party, which was being renovated.
- **Chemiluminescence** tests and **chromatography** reveal that there was first a fire and then an explosion. Further practical experimentation proves the chemicals being used in the renovation caused the explosion, not a bomb.
- After the teeth in the skull of the female victim are correctly repositioned after the blast, they are matched to a missing person named Lisa Winnaker. A swab of her trachea uncovers no trace of carbon from the fire, indicating that she was not breathing when the fire was started, which makes her a murder victim. Semen was also present, indicating a recent sexual encounter. DNA matches that of the judge's son, Antonio.
- The victim's hyoid was cracked and silk fibers around the neck reveal that she was strangled. A split in the cartilage between the T3 and T4 vertebrae and a perforation in the lungs indicate a sharp, thin object punctured the victim's body. It is identified as a stiletto heel, similar to one worn by the judge, implying that she was the murderer.

A state department representative, Alex Radswell, interested in protecting Colombian Judge Ramos, complicates the case for Booth and Brennan in more ways than one. As he is a little person, Booth is uncomfortable around him, particularly since Brennan is rather blunt when it comes to bringing up his lack of stature. Radswell blocks the case at every juncture to ensure the judge's diplomatic immunity is honored and her relationship with the United States is not ill affected. Booth and Brennan are more interested in proving that she murdered a young woman who had been involved with both her son and her husband. Ultimately, Radswell provides the impetus for the judge to waive diplomatic immunity and allow herself to be tried in the U.S. for her crime.

During the investigation, Cam worries that the staff is working too independently and insists that everything is run by her so that she is kept in the loop. Meanwhile, Booth worries that the squints may realize he slept with Cam, and indeed their behavior alerts Hodgins to the possibility, which he immediately shares with Angela.

"The hotel suite was a great set to decorate!" declares set decorator, Kim Wannop with enthusiasm. "I actually dressed the set as it would really have been, burned most of the furniture and

Zack: I also noticed a "broken finger". I'm using those words especially for you, Booth.

Booth: Thanks.

then put it back, before ripping and mangling it up. We even burned a baby grand piano – it was kind of sad to hear all of the strings popping. Everything from the paintings on the walls to the hanging drapes, we burned. That set looked great because of the amount of painting and aging we did to give it a smoked, burnt look. Frayed wires, broken glass and plenty of debris gave it that extra touch of reality."

The suite set was one of the more extreme examples of a crime scene shown in the series. Usually, Wannop is charged with what might seem to be the more mundane task of decorating a suspect's home or workplace. But even a simple space allows for an artistic flair as she is designing for characters with their unique idiosyncrasies. "When dressing for a swing set, character background is most important." Wannop details. "I want the space to feel like the character and represent them as much as possible."

Every set, naturally, starts with the script. Initially Kim reads through the scenes and makes her notes, but this is just the beginning. "We review with the writers some of the qualities of the characters," she notes. "Economic stature is always a question. Do they have money? Are they middle class? We are dealing with stories primarily based on the east coast, which has a different look. We also try to associate the color scheme of the set with the character. The general look that has been established for this show is high-end and high-tech, so we push to maintain that look in other labs, offices, courtrooms, etc."

Chemiluminescence: The emission of light without any heat emission as a result of a chemical reaction.

Chromatography: A laboratory technique used to determine the components within a gaseous or liquid mixture.

THE GIRL WITH THE CURL

WRITTEN BY KARINE ROSENTHAL DIRECTED BY THOMAS J. WRIGHT

GUEST STARRING: KALI ROCHA (JACKIE SWANSON), LISA THORNHILL (KRISTEN MITCHELL), KYLE GALLNER (JEREMY FARRELL), AMANDA CARLIN (DONNA FARRELL), GRACE FULTON (HAILEY FARRELL), MARY GORDON MURRAY (CHARLOTTE CRAFT), BRENT JENNINGS (PLANT SUPERVISOR), JASON MATTHEW SMITH (DAVE SWANSON), JIM HANNA (SECURITY GUARD), ARIEL WINTER (LIZA), MADISON DAVENPORT (MEGAN)

- A young girl's remains are found at a water treatment plant. In life, her hair was bleached, evidence of makeup is present, and she had false teeth to replace her missing **deciduous teeth**. A revised sketch of her image is matched to missing nine year-old Brianna Swanson, who disappeared during the Little Miss Junior Patriot Beauty Pageant.
- A dislocated fracture of the mandible suggests her death was caused by a strong blow to the chin from an object heavy enough to leave markings on her **mental foramen**.
- An ice-cream bar wrapper found with the remains leads investigators to a convenience store near the pageant hotel. Edging on a forestop trammel in the parking lot matches the marks on the victim's chin. The angle and force of the blow reveal that Brianna fell forward and caught her chin, breaking her neck instantly.
- Crushing and scraping injuries to the scapula are congruent with Brianna Swanson being kicked in the back to push her body deeper into a culvert so it would not be seen. Fracture patterns show a slight rotation to the blows, signifying that her attacker suffered from **scoliosis**. Slivers of steel found on the victim are determined to be from tap shoes, indicating another young contestant accidentally killed her and covered up the crime.

When the body of a young girl turns out to be a beauty queen, the team is exposed to the seamier side of child beauty pageants. Though the pageant moms do not come across in the best light, it is one of the young performers who turns out to be the murderer. The accidental death was made worse when she hid the body so she wouldn't miss the pageant.

Booth and Cam continue to dance around the subject of their rekindled affair, feeling out where their new relationship may or may not be heading. When the case is solved and the day is done, Cam waits for Booth so they can leave together, but he prefers to help Bones catch up on paperwork.

In similarly complicated relationship news, Hodgins asks Angela out on a date. At first she says no, but then she changes her answer to prove to both of them that their dating is a bad idea. When the night turns out perfectly, Angela is concerned because she knows when it finally goes wrong it will go really wrong, and so they decide to remain friends.

Angela: ...Childhood should be all about swings.

Zack: Swings?

Angela: Yeah. You know, how high can I go? If I twist the chains, how fast will I spin?

Hodgins: What if I try to jump off before the swing stops?

Angela: Exactly.

Hodgins: I miss that feeling.

Angela: Yeah. Me too.

The episode may end with Angela and Hodgins still single, but their first date is an important milestone of their growing relationship. Both Angela and Hodgins' counterparts Michaela Conlin and TJ Thyne have enjoyed this gentle courtship. "Their relationship has progressed pretty slowly, which I really like," says Conlin. "I hate it when on [other] television shows all of a sudden two people are together. So it's really nice the way they've done it. It's built out of a real chemistry and respect that we have for each other on set as well, which is great. As an actor it's been really, really fun to go on dates and say no and say yes and get pursued and to pursue. It's just a very real relationship."

TJ Thyne agrees that the writers have handled the relationship perfectly. "I have to say, my favorite part of these two being together is that it isn't always easy," he reflects. "One of my favorite episodes this season was the swing episode between Jack and Angela. The months of flirting, that longing to ask her, then finally asking her out, then her saying no, and the heartbreak, then her saying yes, and the pure joy, then the date, then the kiss, ah! That kiss! Then when things couldn't get better, she turns him down. Says she just wants to be friends. Oh man. Jack was just so crushed. Haven't we all been through that? That's what I like most about these two, the true-life emotions. The painful love that isn't always easy to define, and yet it means too much just to let go of it – so worth fighting for."

Deciduous teeth: Baby teeth.

Mental foramen: One of two holes in the front of the mandible (jawbone) that allows passage of the mental nerve and vessels.

Scoliosis: Curvature/deformity of the spine.

'(Shake, Shake, Shake) Shake Your Booty' by KC and the Sunshine Band, *The Best of KC and the Sunshine Band*

'Mona Lisa' by Grant-Lee Phillips, *Virginia Creeper*

THE WOMAN IN THE SAND

WRITTEN BY ELIZABETH BENJAMIN DIRECTED BY KATE WOODS

GUEST STARRING: JOHN MARSHALL JONES (JOE NOLAND), NELSON LEE (SPECIAL AGENT ERIC ZHANG), THEO ROSSI (NICK ARNO), AARON D. SPEARS (AGENT WALT SUGARMAN), JOE CORTESE (LOU MACKEY), KARL MAKINEN (FRANKIE DANIELS), CHAD TODHUNTER (DON MORGAN), SHONTAE SALDANA (MARISOL)

- The body of a federal prosecutor who had been missing for five years is found in the sand outside Las Vegas. Multiple fractures to the skull and upper extremities were caused by something cylindrical, like a baseball bat. Scarab beetles that fed off the body died from ingesting pine oil resin.
- While at the crime scene, circling vultures lead to a female victim, with similar cylindrical injuries to the first victim, killed only a week earlier. The shape of her injuries and the pattern of healing and re-breaking signify a long history of assault. The serial number on her hearing aid leads to the victim's identification as female boxer Wilhelmina "Billie" Morgan. Cortisone on the body had the same deadly effect on the beetles as it did on the first victim.
- Traces of **hexavalent chromium** lead Booth and Brennan to the location of an underground fight club.
- Using a thermal imaging program the squints reconstruct the fight that preceded Billie's death, uncovering a wound that they had missed. Billie was killed by the same bat used on the prosecutor.
- It is determined that the cortisone and the pine oil were both used to treat the **eczema** of the man who buried the bodies. Brennan and Booth convince him to turn over his mob bosses.

After two bodies with possible mob ties are retrieved in Las Vegas, Brennan is ready to head back to the lab to examine them, but Booth is unwilling to let her go. Though he says he needs her help in case more bodies are found, the reluctance has more to do with the gambling addiction he suffers from. He's worried that if left alone in Vegas he will fall off the wagon.

The case leads to an underground fight club where Booth and Brennan go undercover as a "loosely committed couple of hot high rollers with money to burn". When they come across another agent on the inside, Brennan offers Booth's help to maintain the agent's cover by throwing a fight. The rotation is switched, forcing Booth to fight a much larger opponent who is not in on the arrangement. With prompting from Brennan, Booth manages to take the guy down.

While observing the case from the distance of the Jeffersonian, Zack comments that he's never been in a fight in his life. Hodgins, the wise mentor, insults Zack to inspire him to grow angry and force him to throw a punch. The plan works.

Usually Booth and Brennan rely on their brains more often than their brawn. Though both have engaged in physical altercations when necessary, they prefer to exercise restraint. While this certainly is noble for their characters, it can leave the show's stunt coordinator itching for more to do. So, when an episode like 'The Woman in the Sand' comes along, containing four different fight sequences, it really gets stunt coordinator Tim Davison excited.

"Obviously, the main one, David Boreanaz fighting, was our biggest concern," Davison notes. "David had some great insight into how to keep Emily involved in the middle of the fight – they talk between him getting beaten up. It was great incorporating all that into the choreographing of the fight. And the big guy [Monroe] who played David's

Brennan: They call this America's playground?

Booth: We're fifteen miles outside Vegas, Bones. This is America's frying pan.

opponent Troy is a friend of mine; he's a stunt guy who can act. The fact that we had a stunt guy who David got to fight helped a lot, as I didn't have to slip in a stunt double. That entire fight was done with only David and Troy. We really just used the stunt double to design it. David then stepped in and did it all."

Another integral scene to the episode is where the squints recreate the fight the victim was in with the female boxer she actually fought. This was done through a combination of live action and visual effects. "We were very involved with the visual effects." Davison continues. "We designed the whole fight with two girls and we shot it against a white background – they didn't need a green screen. Then the visual effects people digitized it and made it look as if it was built on a computer screen – it was really built off a real fight. It was very clever of the visual effects guys. We've done similar things before with them; we really work hand in hand. Some people think we work against each other, but we don't. We usually work very closely and design things together."

Hexavalent chromium: A chemical used in high-end automotive shops.

Eczema: An inflammation of the skin.

'Viva Las Vegas' by Elvis Presley

'Wolf Like Me' by TV on the Radio, *Return to Cookie Mountain*

ALIENS IN A SPACESHIP

WRITTEN BY JANET TAMARO DIRECTED BY CRAIG ROSS JR.

GUEST STARRING: BENITO MARTINEZ (THOMAS VEGA), JULIE ANN EMERY (JANINE O'CONNELL), CHARLES MESURE (PETE SANDERS), JAMES MCDONNELL (JAMES KENT), SALLI RICHARDSON-WHITFIELD (ASSISTANT U.S. ATTORNEY KIM KURLAND)

- The dehydrated bodies of two adolescent males are found buried in a sealed beer vat. One set of remains shows trauma to the legs, compound fractures, and a pelvis broken in three places. The other is virtually untouched. They are identified as twin brothers Matthew and Ryan Kent, missing for six years.
- The boys were the third victims of the Gravedigger, a serial kidnapper who always follows the same pattern.
- Matthew has signs matching the typical MO of the Gravedigger. Burn marks on the back of the neck are from a stun gun altered to provide a much higher than usual shock to render the victim immobile and affect memory. Ryan has no such wound.
- Both boys' clothing was stained with a sooty residue made up of lead and carbon, **benzene**, and **aldehydes**, suggesting they were taken from an underground parking garage.
- The squints conjecture that Matthew was the intended victim, but Ryan interrupted and the Gravedigger hit him with his car. In the vat, Ryan punctured his own carotid artery to kill himself and hopefully allow his brother to live.
- When Brennan and Hodgins are kidnapped, the team must use all the collected information to find them, though they are unable to identify the Gravedigger.

Booth and Brennan are brought in on the case of the Gravedigger, a kidnapper who buries his victims alive and insists on a ransom being delivered within twenty-four hours. In every case where the ransom was delivered, the victims lived. If not, the victims died. Booth and Brennan interview a kidnap and ransom specialist and a journalist particularly close to the case.

When Hodgins follows Brennan out to the parking structure to share some information, they are both kidnapped by the Gravedigger. In their underground prison Brennan is forced to operate on an injured Hodgins; while Booth scrambles to collect the ransom without success. The abductees manage to hotwire Brennan's cell phone to the car horn so they can send a short text message indicating the type of ground they are buried in. Zack decodes the message and the team finds the burial site.

Hodgins leaves the hospital before being discharged because he wants to catch the Gravedigger by examining the prepaid toll sticker that stuck in his leg when he was struck by the kidnapper's car. Since he is having so much trouble sleeping, Angela reverses her decision not to get involved, telling Hodgins he can stay with her.

Filming the "underground" scenes in this episode provided an interesting challenge for both the actors and the crew.

"We used what's called a 'buck'," explains first assistant director Kent Genzlinger. "Essentially, it's a car that's been cut into pieces. We took a standard vehicle and cut it in half in the middle. Then we had the front of the car with the two front seats that you can shoot from behind, looking out. And we had the rear of the car to look through to the backseat and the back window. We also had a second

Brennan: I'm okay with you thanking God for saving me and Hodgins.

Booth: That's not what I thanked him for. I thanked him for saving... all of us. It was all of us. Every single one. You take one of us away, and you and Hodgins are in that hole forever. And I'm thankful for that.

car where we cut the side doors out, so you could do front to back shots from the sides. So for this episode we had three bucks set up on stage ten."

Emily Deschanel remembers the difficulties she faced as an actor during this episode. "The car wasn't as contained as it seemed," she explains. "A lot of the challenge in doing that episode was really believing that you were in that car all alone. I knew that in reality I could open that door and I'd be fine – I'd be in a soundstage. You have to use your imagination to understand the feeling of being trapped. Then you have to think, what do you do when you're trapped? And what does a character like Brennan do? You would try to get yourself out of there, and use your skills to do that. She's going to do everything she can and use her mind to figure out how to get them out of there."

In order to portray Hodgins' predicament convincingly, TJ Thyne took extra steps to prepare for this situation. "In the days leading up to the shooting of the episode I actually spent a lot of time in that car," he reveals. "I wanted to know every inch of that vehicle, what it felt like to breathe in there, move in there, live in there cramped, crowded and sweaty. I wanted to imagine the pressure on the vehicle itself with all that dirt on top of it – Hodgins would kill me for saying dirt!" he says, laughing. "Damnit TJ, it's agglutinite aridisols!"

Benzene: A toxic liquid obtained from petroleum.

Aldehydes: An organic compound produced by the oxidation of alcohol.

'A Light on a Hill' by Margot & The Nuclear So and So's, *The Dust of Retreat*

'Never Know' by Bob Gentry

'Next to You' by Tim Easton, *Ammunition*

THE HEADLESS WITCH IN THE WOODS

WRITTEN BY KARINE ROSENTHAL & STEPHEN NATHAN
DIRECTED BY TONY WHARMBY

GUEST STARRING: KRISTOFFER POLAHA (WILL HASTINGS), JAKE RICHARDSON (BRIAN ANDREWS), AMANDA FULLER (LORI MUELLER), JOSHUA LEONARD (NATE GIBBONS), TERRELL CLAYTON (DOUG EDISON), MICHAEL TREVINO (GRAHAM HASTINGS)

The ghost of witch Maggie Cinders is said to haunt the woods where the body of student filmmaker Graham Hastings is found. According to legend, she will decapitate anyone who finds her remains. This legend haunts the whole team as they investigate; except for Brennan, who steadfastly refuses to believe in ghosts. She also bluntly reveals that she knows Booth and Cam are romantically involved, and wonders why Booth could not have told her himself. He claims the reason is that he sometimes has trouble communicating with her because as his partner she's almost like a guy, but clearly is not.

Brennan finds common ground with the victim's brother, Will, whose parents died while he was a teen. Unlike her own childhood situation, Will took care of his younger sibling, even dropping out of school so Graham did not have to enter the foster system. As she edges toward a relationship with Will, Booth interrupts a date to arrest him for the murder of his brother. Will lashed out at Graham when he saw how cruel his younger brother had become. He chopped off his brother's head afterward to make it fit with the legend. But the legend possibly proves to be true when a ghostly shape appears on Graham's video. It may just be a reflection... or possibly something more.

Harking back to the hit movie *The Blair Witch Project*, 'The Headless Witch in the Woods' mirrors the idea of a documentary film gone wrong, which leads to an actual murder. In keeping with the visual look of the movie on which this episode is loosely based, director of photography Gordon Lonsdale explains that the second unit filming handled the video filming in exactly the same way as the movie. "It was a handheld camera the whole time,"

Brennan: ...Zack, place some garlic around the remains and chant the Hmong ritual for the preservation of souls.

Zack: Really?

Brennan: This is going to be a long case.

- A decapitated body found deep in the woods is determined to be film student, Graham Hastings, who went missing a year earlier while making a documentary on the Maggie Cinders legend.
- Splinters found in the remains are from a betula uber, a sub species of round leaf birch tree that has been extinct since 1800. Rust flakes on the neck are from an eighteenth-century hand-forged iron.
- The victim's shoulder was dislocated just after death, indicating the body was dragged away from the crime scene. A camera found with the body provides clues to the original crime scene, which leads to the recovery of the murder weapon, the skull — and a second skull.
- The second skull is female and died sometime in the eighteenth or nineteenth centuries. A serial number behind the **occipital condyle** reveals it was stolen from a medical school in an attempt to simulate the head of Maggie Cinders.
- Preliminary tests show only one type of DNA on the ax, but follow-up exams show two, though it's difficult to separate the samples. Glove fragments on the handle are coated with a flame retardant used by firemen — the victim's brother is a fireman. This would also explain why the DNA samples are hard to distinguish: siblings share many of the same chromosomes.

reveals Lonsdale. "We even let the actors hold the cameras sometimes. The camera was like a whole extra character in the show."

The ghost story once again highlights the differences between the empiricist, Brennan, and the spiritual man, Booth. And, like the season one Christmas episode ('The Man in the Fallout Shelter'), Brennan seems to be alone in her strictly scientific viewpoint. This chasm of belief between Booth and Brennan is one of episode-director/co-executive producer Tony Wharmby's favorite facets of the series and this particular episode. "I thought the writers, Stephen Nathan and Karine Rosenthal, did a wonderful job on this episode because it was full of comedy," Wharmby notes. "It had a very comic twist where one character was the believer and the other wasn't. Typically Brennan applied rationale to all these goings-on in the woods, while Booth actually believed them. The script was clever because that issue was the jumping-off point for the episode and it was there right from the get go, in that first scene where they're walking through the woods. There's comedy to exploit in that dynamic, which I think we pulled off. I just loved the story. I thought it was a twist on *Blair Witch*, written extremely skillfully. It's very difficult to write stories that really pay off in the way this one paid off."

Occipital condyle: A protrusion on the occipital bone that forms a joint enabling the head to move relative to the neck.

'Be the One' by Iain Archer, Rick Monroe, and Susan Enan
'Nightbirds' by Ryan Adams, 29

JUDAS ON A POLE

WRITTEN BY HART HANSON DIRECTED BY DAVID DUCHOVNY

GUEST STARRING: RYAN O'NEAL (FATHER TOBY COULTER/MAX KEENAN), LOREN DEAN (RUSS BRENNAN), PATRICIA BELCHER (ASST. U.S. ATTORNEY CAROLINE JULIAN), RYAN CUTRONA (FBI DEPUTY DIRECTOR KIRBY), BARBARA WILLIAMS (BARBARA HARPER), MADISON MASON (JUDGE TED KEMPER), LOU BEATTY, JR. (MARVIN BECKETT), BRYAN CUPRILL (ASST. U.S. ATTORNEY DAN BURRIDGE)

- The body of a middle-aged man is found shot in the head, bound, and burned on the rooftop of a building. The body has a note identifying him as FBI Agent Garrett Delaney and there is a Christopher Columbus coin in his throat.
- Another note with the victim implies that someone was responsible for putting a civil rights activist, Martin Beckett, behind bars for the murder of FBI Agent Gus Harper back in 1978. Additional evidence points to FBI agents being behind the murder. Harper's widow says he kept important evidence in the same safety-deposit box in Ohio that Brennan's parents broke into days after the FBI agent was killed. Special Agent Delaney was Harper's supervisor.
- A list of codenames for bank robbers is found in Harper's files. All the robbers are dead, save Brennan's father. His codename was Columbus.
- The body of Gus Harper is exhumed. A visual examination alone proves that the original autopsy was incorrect about the weapon used in the murder. Enough inconsistencies are present to warrant Beckett's release.
- The bullets used in the murder were from an A1 sniper rifle. A comparison to a list of FBI agents with that training suggests that the sniper was FBI Deputy Director Robert Kirby. He is later found dead in the same manner as Delaney.

Brennan's brother, Russ, shows up after receiving a call from their father warning that they are in danger. When Bones had the case of their father reopened, it reignited interest in him, and them. Father Toby Coulter, a friend of their father's, comes to them with a message to back off, which Brennan ignores. This results in an attempt on Russ's life.

Booth is suspended because his actions in freeing Martin Beckett lead to a media circus. FBI Deputy Director Robert Kirby ultimately proves to be their prime suspect in both an FBI agent's death in the 1970s and the attempt on Russ's life.

When Brennan goes to visit the priest, she realizes that he is, in fact, her father. He gives her the key to a safety-deposit box containing all the evidence to prove the FBI was behind the murder and frame up. Brennan tries to take her father in, but he manages to escape with her brother, Russ.

Meanwhile, Zack presents his doctoral dissertation. It does not go well because of his presentation and deportment. This is also the reason Cam may not hire him – until Angela gives him a makeover.

Due to filming curfews in downtown Los Angeles, the opening scene of the burning body – written as a night scene – had to be filmed in the daytime. "We used a technique that isn't done a lot called 'day for night'," explains co-executive producer Steve Beers. "We went back to an old form of cowboy [movie] photography so we could go up on that roof and make it look like nighttime in the middle of the day. That was fun to figure out. Usually you hide the sky as much as you can when you do day for night. But we were on the rooftop, so instead we had to embrace that."

Another notable scene in this episode was the one in which Assistant U.S. District Attorney Caroline Julian's car is destroyed. Stunt coordinator Tim Davison fondly recalls filming that scene. "We loved that job. I don't know

Booth: I'll take a standup crook over a crooked cop any day of the week.

where they found that car. We set it up to make sure we do the damage and it can't drive off. We put one lug nut on the wheel so the front wheel snaps off. We had the perfect vehicle."

An added element of excitement for the cast and crew for this episode were the familiar names who appeared both in front of and behind the camera. Big screen legend Ryan O'Neal (*Love Story*, *Paper Moon*) came in to play Brennan's father, while acclaimed actor and *The X-Files* star David Duchovny was the episode's director. First A.D. Kent Genzlinger recalls his excitement at O'Neal's appearance on the *Bones* set: "You get a chance in your career to work with certain actors and you get used to stars. But Ryan O'Neal, he's a *legend*." Kent was also in awe of Duchovny's skills as a director: "David Duchovny is very creative and very smart, with a really low key sense of humor. I really enjoyed working with him. He was able to get right into it."

Another famous face on the screen for sharp-eyed viewers to spot was one of the professors on the board reviewing Zack's doctoral thesis – it was the inspiration for the series, Kathy Reichs. "I had a great time. I told Hart Hanson that he may have created a monster," she says, laughing. "Because I really did have a good time."

'Running Up That Hill' by Placebo, *Sleeping with Ghosts*

Practical Experimentation

An important part of the research process of solving crimes is practical experimentation. Clues found in or on a body may not be enough to explain how that victim died. Conjecture can only take a hypothesis so far and is certainly not encouraged in the medico-legal lab of the Jeffersonian. By taking the evidence gathered and placing it in a (hopefully) controlled experiment, investigators can attempt to determine how the events of a crime played out. Doctors Hodgins and Addy particularly enjoy this part of the research process.

Example: During a case where small bone fragments were found on a golf course, it was determined that the body had been frozen, dismembered, and fed through a wood chipper to hide the evidence ('The Man on the Fairway'). Cut marks on the bone were matched to a Black Mannis wood chipper. To determine the dispersal rate of a frozen body fed through the wood chipper, Dr. Hodgins and then-student Zack Addy placed a frozen pig into the chipper so they could determine the width and depth of the distance that the remains would be expelled. Once they knew the area of the chipper's distribution, they were able to approximate the most logical point on the golf course where the machine was placed and determine a search area. In this area they found additional bones samples for further study.

Though the wood chipper test required the extra area of the Jeffersonian parking lot, most tests are contained within the confines of the lab, where strict protocols are maintained to ensure the safety of personnel. Still, no matter how closely scientists follow those safety protocols, there is still an unknown element that can come into play.

Example: When a fire in a hotel suite resulted in an explosion, it was initially unclear if a bomb had been triggered or some other reaction was the cause ('The Girl in Suite 2103'). FBI investigators found no evidence of an explosive charge at the scene; however, the room that was being renovated did have liquor, paint, turpentine, petroleum distillate, and six HVLP canisters inside. Once it was determined the fire was intentionally set, it was only a matter of finding out if those ingredients could cause an explosion. Using careful math, Zack calculated the amount of those ingredients needed to create an explosion approximately 1/1000th the magnitude of the explosion at the hotel. A blast wall was set up to ensure the safety of the scientists, though both Dr. Saroyan and Angela preferred to stay outside the room for the experiment. The ensuing blast, that nearly destroyed the room and knocked Hodgins and Zack off their feet, proved that the mixture was more than enough to have done the damage to the suite.

Naturally, in any experiment conducted during a criminal investigation, priority must be placed on gathering evidence in the most scientific and professional way possible. As that evidence will often be presented in court, it is important that the manner in which the experiment is conducted be above reproach. Any experiment that could be labeled as "goofy science" must be cleared through Dr. Saroyan to ensure that the results are not dismissed out of hand by a jury at a trial.

Example: When the body of a man was found badly burned in a car fire that occurred during a train crash, an experiment was conducted to confirm that extra accelerant was used to increase the intensity of the fire ('The Titan on the Tracks'). Though the experiment did prove successful, the medium used in the experiment was artificial bone covered with spam. Upon hearing the ingredients, Dr. Saroyan immediately shut down the experiment to protect the reputation of the lab.

Subject.

Behind the Scenes With Practical Experimentation

The giddy excitement expressed by Hodgins and Zack when they conduct an experiment onscreen is nothing compared to the joy the crew has setting them up behind the scenes. The technical crew on *Bones* is very much like the scientists on the show – they all enjoy playing with big toys. "When we put the pig through the chipper," co-executive producer Steve Beers recalls, "one of the things that we wanted to do was have a lot of big cups of soda, like Big Gulps. So we had a bunch of guys with Big Gulps watching this pig flying through this chipper. What's more fun? That's a lot of fun."

In creating the experiments, the crewmembers themselves have to figure out exactly how to stage it, much the same way the characters would on the show. Though Zack and Hodgins had been conducting these experiments since early in the first season, it wasn't until the second season opener, 'The Titan on the Tracks', that the crew fully embraced the idea. "We really discovered a certain creative thing about the experiments," Beers admits. "Initially we were planning on building this big fire box. It was going to be quite expensive because we were constructing this thing that technically would be of the same fit and finish as the lab. You know, stainless steel and everything just right."

Though the Jeffersonian may have the funds for the best equipment, *Bones* is on a tighter budget, so the crew have to find alternative ways to run their own tests. "We decided along the way to have a test to see what the spam was going to look like when it burned," Beers continues. "So we just cobbled together this glass cage to burn the spam. When we went down and looked at it, we realized that creatively *that* is what it's all about. Zack and

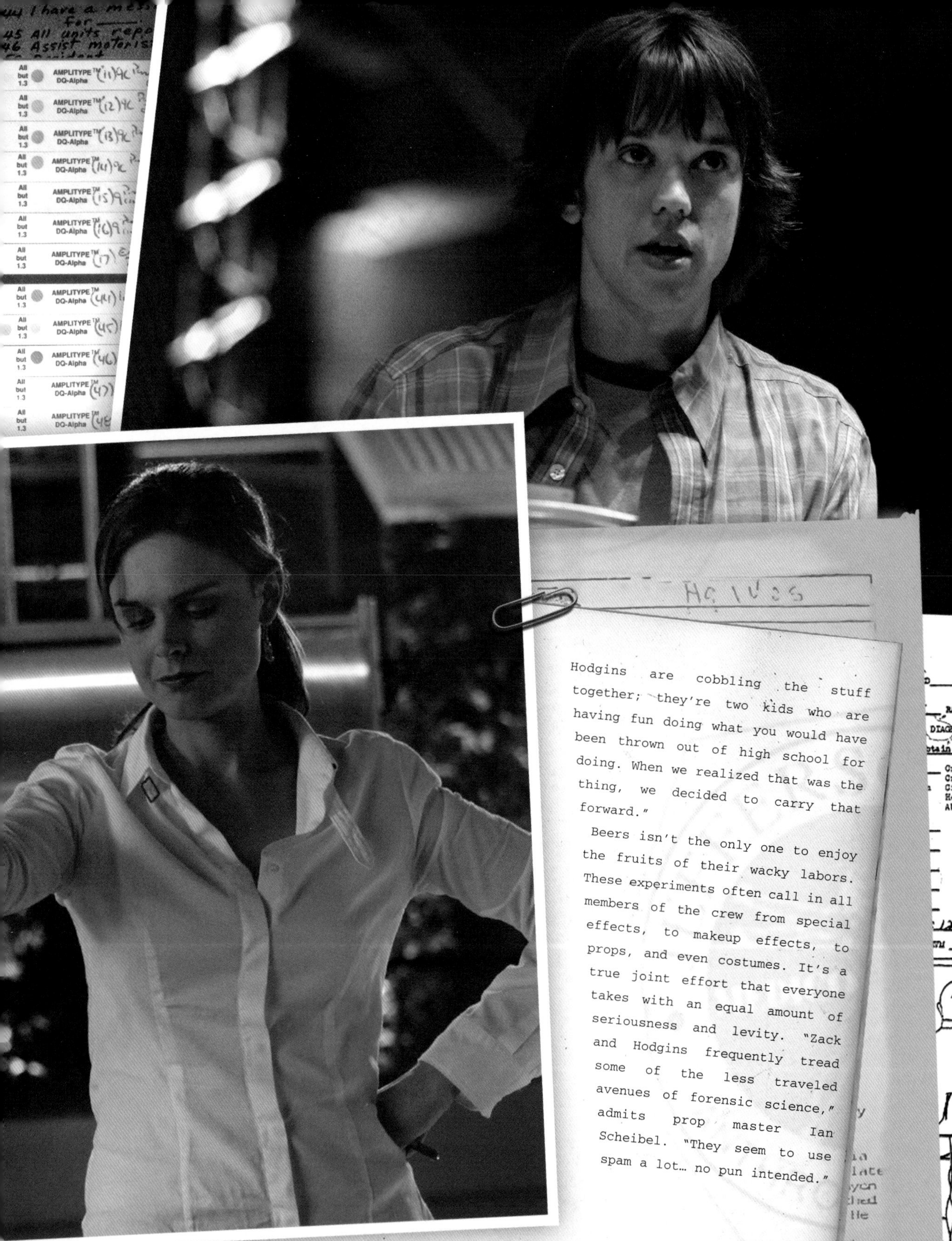

Hodgins are cobbling the stuff together; they're two kids who are having fun doing what you would have been thrown out of high school for doing. When we realized that was the thing, we decided to carry that forward."

Beers isn't the only one to enjoy the fruits of their wacky labors. These experiments often call in all members of the crew from special effects, to makeup effects, to props, and even costumes. It's a true joint effort that everyone takes with an equal amount of seriousness and levity. "Zack and Hodgins frequently tread some of the less traveled avenues of forensic science," admits prop master Ian Scheibel. "They seem to use spam a lot… no pun intended."

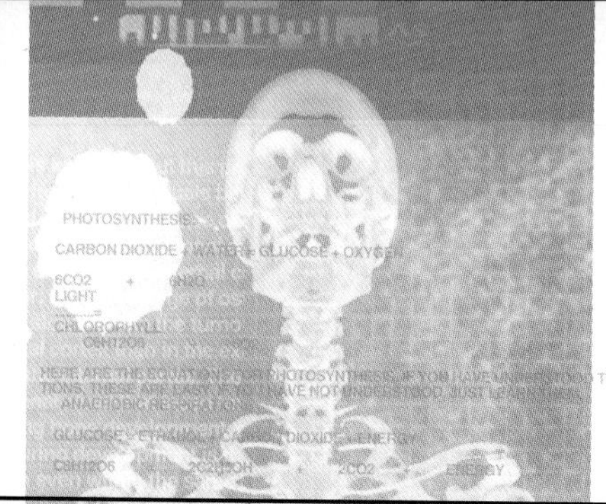

THE MAN IN THE CELL

WRITTEN BY NOAH HAWLEY DIRECTED BY JESÚS SALVADOR TREVIÑO

GUEST STARRING: HEATH FREEMAN (HOWARD EPPS), CHRISTIE LYNN SMITH (CAROLINE EPPS), MIK SCRIBA (WARDEN T.C. EVERETT), PANCHO DEMMINGS (FBI AGENT JAY RAMIREZ), KATHY LAMKIN (MARIANNE EPPS), SANDRA PURPURO (DR. BARBARA YOUNG)

- A fatal fire in the cell of death-row inmate Howard Epps brings Booth and Brennan to the prison, where they quickly determine the charred remains belong to a fireman, not Epps. The serial killer has escaped.
- Epps leads Booth and Brennan to a phone booth where he has left a bone in a vial. Powders in the vial are identified as spices used in Indian food. Knowing that Epp's ex-wife lives above an Indian restaurant Booth and Brennan rush to save her, only to find her severed head frozen solid in a refridgerator.
- A token inserted into the victim's ear for a ride at Hillside Park implies that Epps is going after Booth's son. They find Parker is safe, but has a message from Epps.
- As the autopsy on the head continues, Dr. Saroyan is poisoned when an unidentified dust is released when she skips protocol by not X-raying first and cuts into the skull.
- A small amount of **sodium hydrosulfide** in the ear of the severed head suggests the body is being kept with leather goods. A **Boolean search** of leather goods, combined with the clue left with Parker, leads the team to Parker & Parker Leather Goods. There, they find the body with a sample of the poison. The poison is identified as methyl bromide.

When serial killer Howard Epps escapes from prison he targets Brennan and her co-workers in his latest sick game. Though Brennan finds comfort in her very large gun, everyone is disturbed by the personal attacks. Security at the medico-legal lab is doubled, but Epps still manages to get his dangerous messages through.

When Epps makes contact with Booth's son, Booth demands that Cam ignore protocols while examining the severed head of Caroline Epps. This results in the release of a toxic poison that Cam ingests. An exploding booby trap nearly kills Zack. Booth saves the young forensic anthropologist, while Zack manages to retrieve the poison sample in the process. Hodgins is able to identify the poison, saving Cam.

Brennan and Booth both conclude that they will find Epps waiting in her apartment. Epps is trapped, but attempts to jump over the balcony rather than return to prison. Booth tries to hold onto Epps, but can't – or won't – and the serial killer falls to his death.

Over the course of the first two seasons, *Bones* has presented its viewers with a number of unsettling images, with two of the most disturbing occurring in this episode. First is the severed head of Caroline Epps, which would prove to be a challenge for the makeup effects team, largely because of the tight time factor of television filming.

Makeup effects artist Chris Yagher details the process for creating a severed head, "As soon as possible, we had the actress come in for a life-casting session, during which we took a mold of her head and neck. We then poured up a plaster positive of her likeness and

Zack: My doctor said most of my injuries didn't come from the explosion but from being slammed into the floor. Apparently you're extremely strong.

Brennan: Did you have to be so rough on him?

Booth: It was a bomb. I was being, you know, heroic.

cleaned up the cast. Next, we molded this plaster positive and created a plaster core that is about half an inch smaller than the actress' actual head. By placing this core into the newly created head mold and pouring flesh-tinted silicone between the two, we were able to create a 'skin' of the actress' head and neck. With the skin in the upside-down head mold, polyfoam was then poured into the head cavity, to give the skin an understructure, and capped with hand-fabricated severed-neck tissue. After the head was seamed and painted, realistic teeth were placed into the mouth. A wig made from real human hair was attached to the scalp, and then more human hair was individually punched into the head to create the hairline, eyebrows and eyelashes."

The success of the work was immediately evident when creator/ executive producer Hart Hanson tried to joke around with the end result. "I leaned over to the severed head – I was going to pretend to kiss it," Hanson recalls with a laugh. "I got too close to it and I threw up in my mouth!"

The second disturbing image from the episode was that of Cam doubled over in a seizure as a result of poisoning. This was achieved through Tamara Taylor's own research – and Alka Seltzer. "The foaming of the mouth was Alka Seltzer," Taylor notes. "And Donna Cline, the medical advisor, explained to me how someone having a seizure looks. So I read up a little bit about it and just hoped that it was going to look remotely real."

Sodium hydrosulfide: A chemical compound used in the leather trade for removing hair from hides.

Boolean search: A method of using Boolean Logic (named for English mathematician George Boole) to conduct an advanced search of the internet by imputing specific key words to find a match.

'(What's So Funny 'Bout) Peace, Love, and Understanding?' by Nick Lowe, *Untouched Takeaway*

THE GIRL IN THE GATOR

WRITTEN BY SCOTT WILLIAMS DIRECTED BY ALLAN KROEKER

GUEST STARRING: STEPHEN FRY (DR. GORDON WYATT), EDDIE MCCLINTOCK (SPECIAL AGENT TIM SULLIVAN), ALEX WINTER (MONTE GOLD), EAMONN ROCHE (LLOYD), ERIC JUNGMANN (EDDIE), JOHN LACY (BILL DOWD), JOHN ERIC BENTLEY (PARK RANGER), KELLY KRUGER (ABIGAIL SIMS), JOHN MAYNARD (ICE-CREAM TRUCK DRIVER), FRENCH STEWART (ISAAC HORN)

- The body of a girl is found inside an alligator in the Florida Everglades. After the alligator is sent to the Jeffersonian, the remains of the girl are extracted. A comparison to missing persons reports reveal the victim to be college freshman Judy Dowd.
- Bruising to the victim's vaginal wall suggests she was raped. A puncture mark above her scapula provides the cause of death. Ridge marks in the wound resemble the threads of a screw, suggesting she was impaled on one.
- Photos from the victim's spring-break vacation show that she was filmed for a website that specializes in shirtless shots of drunken college girls. Interviews with the proprietor of the website, Monte Gold, and a preacher who follows the tour bus around are conducted.
- **Cryptosporidium** on the victim's clothes from saw grass indicates that the original crime scene is two miles south of where the body was found.
- The driver of the website tour bus says that Gold forced himself on the girl and she wanted off the bus afterwards. When Gold is found dead, it is determined that the victim's father killed him.
- Blood on the threads of an exposed gearshift in the preacher's truck matches the victim, indicating he killed her after picking her up from the tour bus.

When music from an ice-cream truck annoys Booth to the point where he shoots the clown speaker on its roof, he is taken off duty and required to speak with the department psychiatrist, Dr. Wyatt. With Booth out of commission, FBI Special Agent Tim "Sully" Sullivan is assigned to the case with Brennan. At first, she doesn't know what to make of her temporary partner, but when the case is over they agree to go out on a date.

Booth doesn't feel that he needs to speak with Dr. Wyatt, but the psychiatrist refuses to sign off on him before they talk about what he did. They eventually come around to the fact that Booth is not sure if serial killer Howard Epps slipped from his hand or if he let go. Although Wyatt does sign the forms reinstating Booth, the two will continue to meet.

Now that he has a doctorate and a position of authority, Zack is having trouble communicating with Angela as her superior, because he's acting superior. Once they get past the initial tension, Angela has her own problems when she silently confirms the identity of their suspect to the victim's father who, in turn, kills the man.

"That was a tipping point for Booth," David Boreanaz says, regarding his character's role in the death of serial killer Howard Epps in the prior episode ('The Man in the Cell'). "That was something that just kind of put Booth over the edge with a lot of stuff that had been building in his life. When you get to a second season with a show, you're able to get more into the back-story of the characters, which I always think is more interesting than the procedural stuff."

The back-story had already established

Sully: ...You're telling me you're just gonna be a bone lady your whole life?

Brennan: I spent years studying anthropology.

Sully: Well, I got a degree. But I'm not gonna let it ruin my life.

that as a sniper Booth had killed close to fifty people, but this was different. "In this instance we were thinking: what if Booth honestly didn't know whether or not he had allowed Epps to die?" says Hart Hanson. "Did he execute this guy? Did he drop him or did he lose his grip on him? He knew why he'd killed everyone he'd ever killed before: it was his job; it was his duty. Even if he hated it, as in the Iraq show ('The Soldier on the Grave'), he would do his duty. We just thought it would be interesting to explore how a guy copes with that."

Of course, Hanson being Hanson, there had to be a lighter comic reason behind the episode as well. "We wanted this Gary Cooper character in therapy," he explains with a smile. "That was just funny: he was the last guy in the world who would ever go to therapy. It was fun to think: what therapist in the world would get through to Booth? Initially the idea was to have a great big male presence, like a fatherly presence – an alpha male that even Booth would have to adjust to. But then we had the idea of Stephen Fry, probably because of Hugh Laurie on *House*, as they used to be comedy partners. When we approached him, much to my shock, Stephen jumped at the chance to do it. And I think, one of our best pairings on television is Stephen Fry as a therapist and David Boreanaz in therapy."

Cryptosporidium: A water-borne protozoan parasite.

'When I Hear Music' by Debbie Deb, *She's Back*

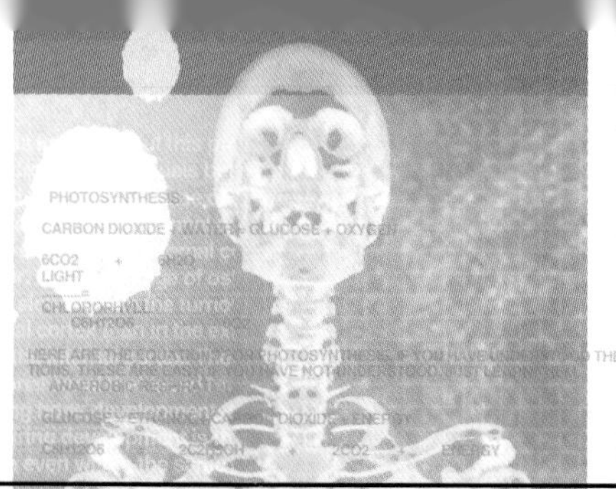

THE MAN IN THE MANSION

WRITTEN BY CHRISTOPHER AMBROSE DIRECTED BY DWIGHT LITTLE

GUEST STARRING: STEPHEN FRY (DR. GORDON WYATT), EDDIE MCCLINTOCK (SPECIAL AGENT TIM SULLIVAN), REID SCOTT (ROBERT FRAZIER), PATRICIA BELCHER (CAROLINE JULIAN), ERNIE HUDSON (DAVID BARRON), MERIDITH MONROE (CLARISSA BANCROFT), JESSE D. GOINS (JUDGE), PETER PARROS (OFFICER) JAMES EARL (TEENAGER), JAMES HIROYUKI LIAO (MEDICAL EXAMINER), ERIN TORPEY (WOMAN #1), AZITA GHANIZADA (WOMAN #2)

- The body of Terrance Bancroft is found in the den of his mansion, bound to a chair and with multiple stab wounds.
- Prior to his death he had caught one of the kids at a youth center where he volunteered in possession of a large amount of heroin, presumably acting as a drug mule. Blood matching Bancroft's is found on a sweatshirt in the kid's locker. Local police find the boy had been killed, execution style, twenty days earlier.
- **Calliphora vomitoria** with Bancroft's body indicates he had been dead eighteen-and-a-half days, meaning someone had to have placed his blood on the boy's sweatshirt to frame him.
- A fungus is found on Bancroft's interior cervical vertebrae, signifying that the blood pooled while he was on his back for several hours. The murderer returned later, forcing the body into the chair and stabbing him fourteen more times to make it look like a home invasion.
- A fiber in the victim's throat is determined to be muskrat hair that matches a jacket worn by the director of the youth center, Robert Frazier.
- The fungus matches an infection found in the suspect. When the suspect punctured the victim's jugular he nicked himself, introducing the bacteria directly into the victim's blood stream, and linking himself to the murder.

The legal case nearly gets kicked when Hodgins does not reveal that the victim was once his best friend. The team must race to find additional evidence that he has not touched, while Jack turns in his resignation. He manages to keep his job when the case is won, but Hodgins makes sure that Booth knows what he did so they can move past it.

Booth considers himself under evaluation by Dr. Wyatt, though truthfully he's in therapy. At the doctor's suggestion, Booth changes his wacky ties and wild socks for more traditional clothing because they are seen as a quiet rebellion that keep him from accessing his deeper issues. One of the issues that Booth has is with people who are entitled, as this case brings out. He eventually changes back to his usual look after learning something valuable about himself.

Brennan worries that something is wrong when Sully is reluctant to move their relationship to the next level. At the same time, he's worried about moving too fast and goes to Booth for advice – which is awkward for both of them.

"David and I have gotten to do a lot of fun scenes together recently," says TJ Thyne, regarding how Booth and Hodgins have developed a closer working relationship over the second season. "I hope that continues. I think the dynamic between Jack and Booth is a lot of fun to watch. I mean they are both really confident in who they are and what they do, and yet completely different in how they go about handling relationships and situations. Isn't that what you find in your group of friends? Don't you love that person that sees

Hodgins: I'm saving Dr. Saroyan the trouble of firing me.

Brennan: Well, how much trouble is it? "You're fired." That's no trouble at all. A child could do it.

Saroyan: [to Hodgins] I appreciate it.

things completely differently from you? Look how these two differ even in their way of dealing with the women in their lives. They could get into a great debate about it – probably have, many times." At the end of this episode, Hodgins, realizing the kind of guy Booth is, uses his resignation as an apology to get their friendship back on track.

On a less pleasant note, the opening scene of the episode has Booth and Brennan warned about the high volume of flies attracted to the dead body they have come to investigate. Insects, maggots, and rodents are in full supply over the course of the series, though prop master Ian Scheibel finds that part of his job easier than one might imagine. "It's not difficult for me at all," he says. "For live bugs and other animals I pick up the phone and call Brockett's Film Fauna and tell them how many maggots and rats I want and what their call time is. Occasionally, the script will be very specific and we will need *sphecius speciosus* [killer wasps], a *tibicen lyricen* [large cicada] or a third instar *phaenicia sericata* [green bottle fly] and I will call Professor Raupp at the Entomology Department, University of Maryland, to get a specimen or two. Previously deceased, of course."

Calliphora vomitoria: A common blow fly known as the blue bottle fly, found in most areas of the world.

'Tears and Laughter' by John Czerwick
'Twilight Zone' by Golden Earring, *The Continuing Story of Radar Love*

BODIES IN THE BOOK

WRITTEN BY KARINE ROSENTHAL DIRECTED BY CRAIG ROSS JR.

GUEST STARRING: EDDIE MCCLINTOCK (SPECIAL AGENT TIM SULLIVAN), JONATHAN SLAVIN (HANK), VALARIE PETTIFORD (ELLEN LASKOW), CHRIS CONNER (OLIVER LAURIER), COLBY FRENCH (GREG BRALEY), STEVEN BRAUN (ASHTON KELLER), DARBY STANCHFIELD (CONNIE LOPATA)

- A body is found in a marina tied to the chain of an anchor with red tape, in a manner matching a murder in Brennan's latest book. Cause of death was a gunshot. A sketch compared to DMV records matches Jim Lopata. The killer is initially suspected to be the victim's brother-in-law, angry that his sister was being abused by her husband, but he proves to have an alibi.
- The body of Sadie Keller is found in a pet shop being eaten by rats in a glass cage, also like in Brennan's book. She was tied with the same tape as the first victim and also died from a gunshot. Though her husband was fed up with her wild life style and stands to inherit a substantial amount of money, he was out of town on the night of the murder.
- A trail of fire ants leads Booth and Brennan to a third victim, Brennan's publicist, Ellen. She also died from a gunshot in a manner matching a murder in Brennan's book. Though the tape and bullets were the same in each case, the specifics of each attack were different.
- Clues lead Booth and Brennan to realize that the suspects in each of the first two cases conspired with the publicist's assistant. They each committed a murder for one another so they would all have alibis. They were united as members of internet chat rooms devoted to Dr. Brennan.

While publicizing her latest book, Bones is shocked to find bodies turning up killed in the exact same manner as they died in her fiction. Though Brennan is initially reluctant to believe they're linked, Sully wants in on the investigation so he can help protect her. As more bodies are found, Brennan begins to feel responsible for the deaths. She wonders if she hadn't written the scenes, the people wouldn't have died. The case introduces tension to Brennan and Sully's relationship because of his over-protectiveness. Brennan tries to push him away, but Booth helps her see that Sully is one of the good guys.

After Sully reviews Brennan's fan mail, Booth goes to see her number one obsessed fan, Oliver Laurier, whom he met back when he first started working with Bones ('Pilot'). Laurier leads them to a mystery books chat room and the "Brennanites", who are her devoted fans. Laurier quickly casts doubt on the idea that he is the killer when he faints at the sight of his own blood. Other Brennanites do turn out to be the murderers, working together to take care of each other's problems, while allowing for their own alibis.

The writers approach each episode of *Bones* by first determining how the body will be found and then building the case around that image. Though they usually strive for realism, 'Bodies in the Book' gave them a chance to have some fun. "We actually went overboard because the bodies are from her novel," creator/executive producer Hart Hanson explains. "Someone is copy-catting her novel. So, in a way, it's mocking her fiction writing. We tend to be real, but push the limits. These bodies… no one would kill anyone this way. We just had a good time. So it's a bit of a heightened reality, but still plausible."

All was not fun and games in this episode, however, when the makeup effects team faced an unexpected challenge. Chris Yagher explains: "The producers and I discussed how we would create the body of Ellen Laskow,

Cam: Just remember, at the end of your books, Kathy Reichs always gets the murderer.

the dead woman being eaten by fire ants. We determined that an actress would need to be found that matched a body we had in our inventory, namely a Caucasian female with dark brown hair. While prepping the body, I found out that because of a miscommunication, the director cast an African American female with light-brown cornrows.

"With about four days left before shooting, we quickly found a head and two arms that resembled those of the newly-cast actress, attached them to the body that we were already preparing, and re-created the ant bite marks that had previously been made on the Caucasian female's face and arms. We then approached the hair department and acquired the cornrow wig and hair extensions to complete the look. After a few late nights, we completed the body and arrived on time for the filming of the scene."

'Fault Line' by Black Rebel Motorcycle Club, *Howl*
'The Secret Sun' by Jesse Harris and The Ferdinandos, *The Secret Sun*

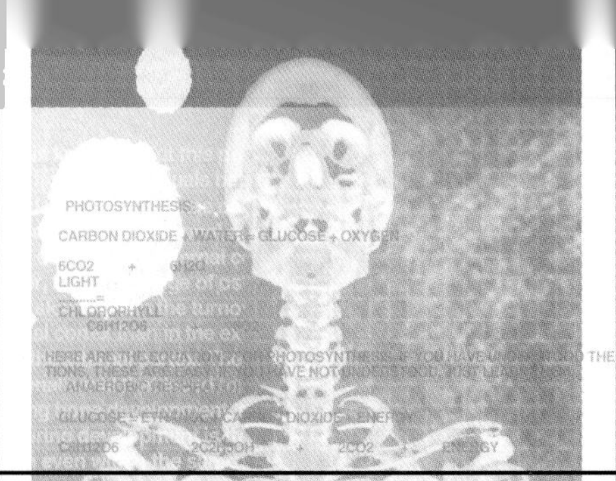

THE BONELESS BRIDE IN THE RIVER

WRITTEN BY GARY GLASBERG *DIRECTED BY* TONY WHARMBY

GUEST STARRING: EDDIE MCCLINTOCK (SPECIAL AGENT TIM SULLIVAN), MICHAEL PAUL CHAN (PROFESSOR SHI JON CHEN), JP PITOC (DREW HARPER), JAMES HONG (JOSEPH HAN), DEBORAH THEAKER (JACKIE BURROWS), LUCILLE SOONG (MAI ZHANG), ERIC STONESTREET (OFFICER)

Brennan tries to vacation with Sully, but Booth keeps interrupting to bring her in on a case. Eventually, Brennan and Sully offer to help, if only to solve the case so they can enjoy their vacation on the boat he is thinking about buying.

The case centers on a Chinese ritual known as minghun: an ancient belief that if an unmarried male dies, his family should rebury his bones with the bones of a woman, in a form of marriage. When the original fiancé of the murdered mail-order bride claims that he received his money back when he rejected her, suspicion falls on the proprieter of the service. When she was rejected the woman poisoned the girl and collected money for her bones to make up for the loss.

Sully buys the boat and asks Brennan to sail off with him for a year. She goes to Booth for his opinion and, though he's condescending, he ultimately tells her to take the trip. Rationally, she knows she should go, but she can't. When she goes to see Sully off on his boat, named Temperance, Booth is right there with her.

One of the highlights of this episode is a chase between Booth and a suspect that goes across rooftops and alleys, providing a fun challenge for stunt coordinator Tim Davison. "We wanted to do what's known as a 'free running' sequence, which is this new sport," he explains. "We went and found this alley where we could jump across this and that, and then set dressing got involved and brought me all sorts of set pieces. The whole company got together and we came up with a sequence that they seemed to be very happy with. I got a guy that had done Cirque du Soleil – the perfect type of athlete for that sort of thing. We were going to put him on wires but we never had to because this kid was so talented. He jumped from the building and he slid down on his hands,

Brennan: What exactly do you have to contend with on the job that I don't?

Booth: You, Bones. You don't have to contend with you.

- A trunk containing the skin of a woman is found in a river. Brennan has it brought back to the lab.
- Cam confirms that the skeleton was removed after incisions were made along the body and it was boiled. Angela cannot create a skull but can tell that the victim was Asian.
- Algae in the trunk is identified as **microcystis aeruginosa**. The size of the scum colony indicates the trunk was submerged for eight days.
- A piece of a **patella** is found in the fatty tissue of the leg. A square rather than triangular shape suggests that she had **Fong disease**, which could signify that the victim grew up in a non-industrialized, rural environment, common in rural Asia.
- An attempt at a victim sketch combined with a partial print gets a hit off the Homeland Security site, identifying the victim as Li Ling Fan. She entered the country on a fiancée visa from China, and is discovered to be a mail-order bride.
- Evidence of toxicity damage to the kidney shows she was poisoned. Toxicology identifies the toxin as a root called Lei Gong Den, which is deadly in large doses.
- The poison is found in the refrigerator of the woman who owns the mail-order bride service that brought the victim to America.

and he ran through the alley and leapt through the scaffolding and all that stuff. We were able to do that all practically and never had to put him on a wire."

Meanwhile, one of the less successful aspects of this episode would have to be the ill-conceived experiment Zack and Hodgins perform in a misguided attempt at a facial reconstruction without a skull. "According to the script, the head needed to be separated from the body and then inflated," make-up effects atist Chris Yagher explains. "These requirements came with a set of unknowns that we had to work through in order to determine what materials would work the best, how we would construct and reinforce the body, and how we would structure the head so that it could be inflated and deflated several times on set and still look realistic. This last unknown came with another variable, namely the pressure expelled by the air tank into the head. While on set we found that we could not adequately control the air pressure and we ended up splitting the head open on two separate occasions. After some scrambling, what we found is that sometimes the simplest solutions work the best: we put our lips on the air tube and blew."

Microcystis aeruginosa: A common species of cyanobacteria (often called blue-green algae) that live in water and obtain their own energy through photosynthesis.

Patella: Knee cap

Fong disease: Also Nail-Patella Syndrome, it is a rare genetic disorder mostly exhibited in poorly developed fingernails, toenails, and patellae.

'Running Up That Hill' by Placebo, *Sleeping with Ghosts* (bonus track)

'You' by Fisher, *The Lovely Years*

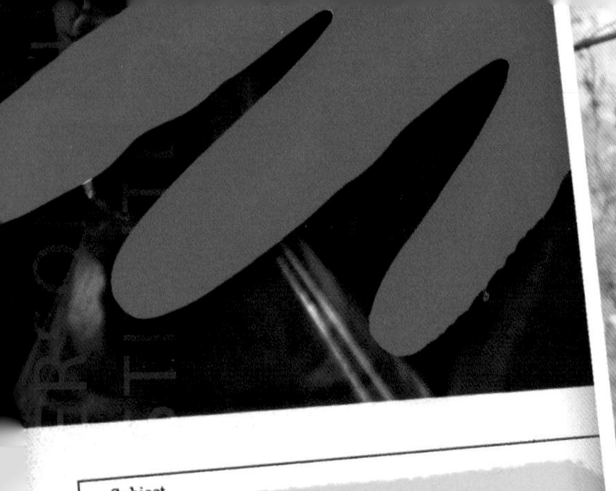

Subject.

Identifying Foreign Matter

An important component of any forensic investigation is identifying foreign matter within a body. Though a generic term, "foreign matter" can refer to any object that simply does not naturally occur in humans. These objects can be key in determining important information about the deceased. Serial numbers on implants, for example, can lead to an identity of a victim. While a piece of a murder weapon that has become lodged in the body of a victim can provide a key clue to catching a murderer.

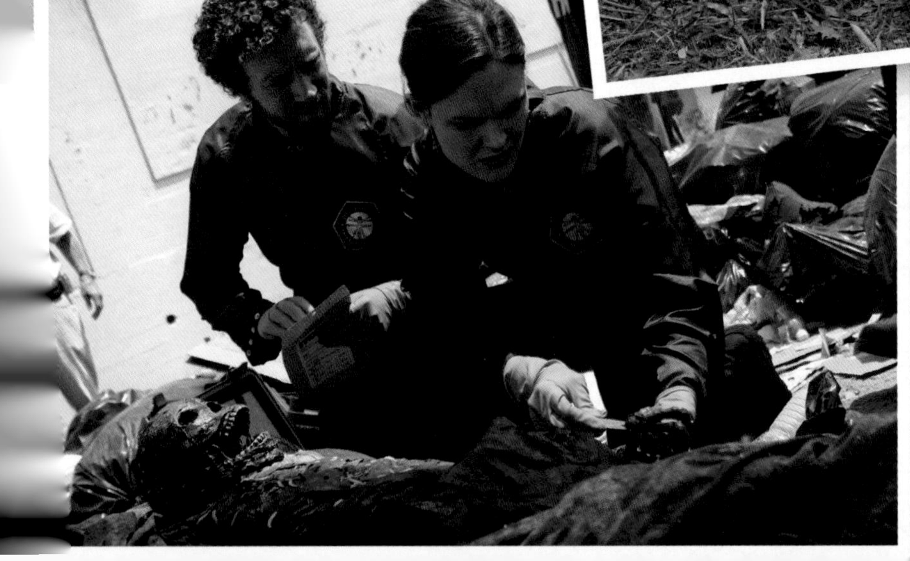

Detecting Foreign Matter

The primary way to conduct a search for any foreign matter is a simple visual examination of the remains. This would include both exams conducted by the naked eye as well as X-rays, as either method used exclusively could miss a clue.

Evidence from the Attacker

The most useful evidence in a murder investigation can be that which comes from the attacker. In a physical fight, skin found under the victim's fingernails can lead to a DNA match, as well as blood on the victim, hair, semen, etc. It is also possible for evidence to transfer into the body of a victim from a weapon's point of entry. In an extremely rare example, a woman bit off the ear of her attacker. That ear was found in the deceased's larynx, which not only helped in identifying her attacker, but chemicals found in the ear helped pinpoint the location of her kidnapped son ('The Woman in the Car').

Toxicology and Chemical Tests

Toxicology tests on blood, tissue and the organs of a body can be used to determine if the victim was poisoned, as well as identifying that poison. Chemical tests can also be run to determine if the subject was on any form of medication that could indicate a medical condition or drug abuse – providing the investigation with further clues about the victim.

Osteological Profiles

An osteological profile can be conducted for a more intensive examination of the bone makeup, which will provide information that a simple blood or tissue test may overlook. For example, traces of lead and nickel in the profile of a man dead since the 1950s indicated that he was a coin collector ('The Man in the Fallout Shelter'). This type of workup is very much the specialty of the forensic anthropologist.

Laser-Induced Breakdown Spectroscopy

This process provides an elemental analysis of the deceased. The process uses a highly energized laser pulse to analyze matter, whether it be solid, liquid or gas. This can be particularly useful in providing a detailed analysis of the chemical makeup of a body to pinpoint environmental factors that could indicate where a person lived ('The Graft in the Girl').

THE PRIEST IN THE CHURCHYARD

WRITTEN BY LYLA OLIVER   DIRECTED BY SCOTT LAUTANEN

GUEST STARRING: STEPHEN FRY (DR. GORDON WYATT), GEORGE COE (FATHER WILLIAM DONLAN), DAVID BURKE (FATHER MATTHEW SANDS), WENDY BRAUN (LORRAINE BERGIN), JOHNNY LEWIS (ENZO FALCINELLA), SOREN FULTON (JAMES LEVAY)

- Flooding in a church cemetery unearths the body of a man buried three years earlier, though the last official burial in the cemetery occurred in 1951. The victim has evidence of trauma to the frontal bone. Cause of death is initially believed to have been cranial cerebral trauma.
- A sketch of the victim is not initially recognized at the church, until a former altar boy identifies it as resembling Father McCourt. The priest had left the church three years earlier; disappearing and leaving only a note saying he was leaving the priesthood.
- Unexplained greenstick fractures on the victim's left ulna, fibula, and some ribs seem to have occurred after death, when he was dragged for burial, due to the fact that the matrix of the bone was weakened as a result of **taxin** poisoning. The poison ultimately proves to have been the cause of death.
- Tiny silver fragments embedded in the victim's skull are matched to the chalice used for the sacramental wine. The victim was struck after death.
- Lorraine, the parish administrator confesses to killing McCourt and poisoning a second priest because she suspected them both of inappropriate relations with young boys. She only wanted to make McCourt sick, but he fell and hit his head. She struck him with the chalice to make sure he was dead before she buried him.

Booth and Brennan's banter is far more strained than usual and Booth feels that issues affecting their working relationship are causing Bones to lash out at his belief system. He insists that they both go and see his therapist. Dr. Wyatt believes that they both think that Brennan didn't sail off with Sully because of Booth. The doctor sets their minds at ease by explaining that Brennan was simply not ready to lead a purposeless life at this time. Meanwhile, Booth was taking credit for something that had nothing to do with him.

Angela seeks out Wyatt for similar relationship advice. Hodgins has asked her to move in with him, but she's not ready for the commitment. The doctor's words give her the support she needs to stick to her decision. Angela also calls Wyatt out, suspecting that he lied to Booth and Brennan about their problems because as an FBI psychiatrist his job is to ensure that the agents get back into the field.

Once again, the subject of religion cuts right to the heart of the differences between the Booth and Brennan. This time, the case opens up the subject in a way that provides them with a release valve to deal with Sully's departure and what it means for their relationship. "These characters are completely polarized in the way they view the world," Hart Hanson reminds us. "And with any case they get into, they're going to have different views of the suspects, the crime – whatever the theme of the show is. That kind of generates itself. We often have to stop ourselves from going too far in that direction and forgetting about the crime. We could go away from the tease and write a whole show about them arguing over the topic!"

The writers often focus on religion as a central issue because it allows the

Brennan: Can't you just be satisfied that if I'm wrong about God, I'll burn in hell?

Booth: That's tempting.

Brennan: Good. Now how about we get back to work?

discussion to branch off in different areas. "We touch on faith and belief in God a lot on this show," says Hanson, "because when you have someone who only believes in what is palpable and tangible, it's just going to come up. The discussion about faith in people and faith in God, all that."

Stephen Nathan adds, "And then, towards the end of this year, we even started dealing with the question of what is love and romance. To Brennan it's a chemical reaction, while Booth, he believes it's something in your soul."

David Boreanaz agrees that this is an essential aspect of the show. "With the discussion come the arguments," he reflects, "which bring out our relationship even more. Both characters have strong points of views on certain things and are not afraid to share them. I think that's what defines our show."

In the end, these arguments only serve to point out what is so obvious to the audience – and to Angela. It is the crux of the problem in this episode, though neither Booth nor Brennan can bring themselves to admit it. Emily Deschanel, however, can easily pinpoint it for her character. "She's realizing that not all people abandon you. And not all people disappoint you and leave. When Sully leaves and Brennan's waving goodbye to him, there's Booth right behind her to comfort her. He knows exactly what to say to cheer her up."

Taxin: A poison derived from boiling yew tree needles. Yew trees are often found in church graveyards as a symbol of sadness.

'The Time Comes' by Nina Gordon, *Bleeding Heart Graffiti*
'Slow Dance' by John Legend, *Once Again*

THE KILLER IN THE CONCRETE

WRITTEN BY DEAN WIDENMANN DIRECTED BY JEFF WOOLNOUGH

GUEST STARRING: RYAN O'NEAL (MAX KEENAN), GREG BAKER (MELVIN GALLAGHER), PHILLIP RHYS (CLARK LIGHTNER), DALIA PHILLIPS (VELESKA MILLER), TOM EVERETT (HUGH KENNEDY), DEREK WEBSTER (OFFICER), BILL ESCUDIER (TIM)

• Bones are found in a section of concrete at a federal flood abatement project. The concrete is sent to the Jeffersonian where the bones can be safely separated for examination. A facial reconstruction identifies the victim as Billy Rae McKenna, a suspected mob hit man.

• A small hole in the back of the cranium suggests an ice pick was the cause of death. The pick entered the **medullary pyramids** where beveling on the entry site suggests it was wiggled to paralyze the victim, but allowed him to live for upwards of several hours. Chunks of concrete in the shape of a sinus cavity and bronchial tubes indicate the concrete was poured over the victim while he was still alive.

• The method of death implies another hit man, Hugh Kennedy, was the murderer. He and the victim were both employees of crime boss Melvin Gallagher. Shortly after McKenna's death, Kennedy was killed in an explosion while fleeing a bail enforcement agent. All that was left of him was a severed leg. An examination of the leg shows it was severed cleanly at a ninety-degree angle and there are kerf marks in the wound, suggesting it was amputated with a saw, not in an explosion, meaning that Kennedy is still alive. Booth finds the missing murderer, but the man escapes.

Brennan's father, Max, pays his daughter a couple of visits, asking her to look at his rap sheet in the hope that she will understand him better. Booth examines the file and confirms that Max had only killed bad men. Though Booth still intends to arrest Max, he suggests that Brennan should forgive her father.

In the course of the investigation, Booth locates the suspect, but the man gets the drop on Booth and leaves him bound in a hotel room. A crime boss searching for the hit man finds Booth and kidnaps him, attempting to force Booth to admit that the hit man is still alive.

Brennan goes to her father for help and they track Booth back to the hotel room. Max determines that the crime boss, Gallagher, has Booth. With the help of the squints, Brennan finds a clue to Booth's location, calls it in to the FBI, and goes after him with her father. Max and Brennan rescue Booth, but Max takes off in Brennan's car before he can be arrested. Max leaves the car in her garage with a message that he still wants to talk to her about her mother.

Shades of 'Aliens in a Spaceship' can be seen in this episode when the squints rally to save a member of the team. This time, it's Booth, not Brennan, who needs rescuing. Although putting the main characters in jeopardy heightens the drama of the series, it is something that Hart Hanson does not do willingly. "I told Emily Deschanel at the beginning," he explains, "'Once a year, you will be in danger and Booth will rescue you.' I always resist those stories, and it's turned out to be quite good. Then, in this episode, there's the flipside when she comes to rescue him, which is only fair."

Cop: And when we dug up the cement —

Brennan: No, that's concrete. Cement is an ingredient in concrete.

Booth: Yeah, that's a real important distinction to make at this juncture.

One of the goals of the series has always been to highlight the work of these amazing scientists. In this way, it differs from a traditional procedural drama because, while the mystery is important, it is the science that is often the focus. This episode brings that idea to the forefront when the team loses the FBI agent – the man who interprets the information they process. Left on their own, the squints aren't sure they can solve the crime – but they do.

The science of the squints is something that the producers take very seriously. Executive producer Barry Josephson is proud to note that that aspect of the show is a key component in the success of the series: "Hart got a letter from a fifteen year-old girl that said, 'I want to grow up and be a forensic anthropologist.' That was very exciting to me because I always said to Hart – when we were conceiving the lab and Brennan's character – that I was hopeful that kids and college students would watch this show and say, 'I want to be that person,' because that's not something that's on TV. When he showed me that letter, I was thrilled. And I'm thrilled to see that on the internet message boards and the blogs people are saying this is a world of science that they haven't seen before. That part of it is really rewarding."

Medullary pyramids: Also known as renal pyramids — any of the various pyramidal masses seen upon the longitudinal section of the kidney that contain part of the secreting tubules and the collecting tubules.

'Shipwrecked' by Shane Alexander, *Stargazer*
'Hold on to You' by Marjorie Fair, *Self Help Serenade*
'Keep on Trying' by Poco, *The Ultimate Collection*

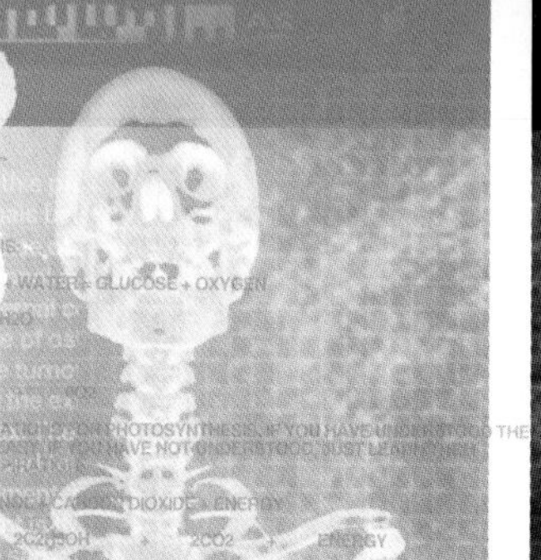

SPACEMAN IN A CRATER

WRITTEN BY ELIZABETH BENJAMIN DIRECTED BY JEANNOT SZWARC

GUEST STARRING: ANDREA THOMPSON (NINA SANBORN), LISA WALTZ (JEAN MARIE HOWARD), IAN ANTHONY DALE (COMMANDER JAMES ADAMS), GLENN MORSHOWER (COL. BOB REID), SARAH BLOOM (COLLEEN ADAMS), JUDITH MORELAND (LONI GOWAN), ROB BROWNSTEIN (DR. HENRY PASCAL), MICHAEL RODRICK (ADAM BAHR), EJ CALLAHAN (FARMER)

- A body drops out of the sky, leaving a crater on impact. From the decimated state of the body, it is determined that the victim fell from a minimum of 1200 feet. Presumably, he was pushed out of a plane.
- Areas of **radiolucence** on the X-ray reveal extremely porous bone, showing significant demineralization that suggests the victim suffered bone loss during space travel. The victim's legs, hips and lower vertebrae have suffered over twenty percent demineralization, which signifies that the victim spent ten months in space. The body is determined to be Colonel Calvin Howard of the National Space Agency.
- Signs of trauma to the bones that match with slashes in the victim's clothing prove the murder weapon was a curved blade approximately sixty-five millimeters thick. An estimate of blade velocity suggests it was moving at 260 miles per hour. It is determined that the victim was pushed through a propeller blade that was idling.
- Damage to the propeller on the plane of astronaut trainee, James Adams, indicates that he was involved in the murder. Adams admits that, after Howard told them that he was planning on going back into space in place of Adams, his wife slapped the victim, accidentally pushing him into the propeller.

In a case that hints at little green (or gray) men, everyone is having fun at Hodgins' expense, until evidence points to the victim having spent time in space. It turns out the origin of the body is more terrestrial than extra. Stone-walling by the National Space Agency makes the case more difficult to investigate as Booth and Brennan interview astronauts, their wives, and true believers from the "tinfoil hat" society who are searching for evidence that aliens walk among us.

Meanwhile, Hodgins goes to Booth for advice on proposing as he's looking for the right way to ask Angela to marry him – she has already said no to him once. He winds up taking her out for a fancy dinner and proposing in a traditional manner. Angela surprises them both by saying no, even though she admits that she does love him.

The original rejected marriage proposal that Hodgins mentions during this episode had not been seen at the time 'Spaceman in a Crater' aired. The proposal took place during the episode 'Player Under Pressure', which was scheduled to air on 18 April 2007. The episode was pulled in light of the tragedy at Virginia Tech two days earlier, in which an armed man killed thirty-two fellow students and faculty members. Though the storyline of the episode was vastly different from the real life situation, the similarities of a murder on a college campus made it seem inappropriate to air at the time. Fox pulled the episode, instead running a repeat of 'Aliens in a Spaceship'. The network had stated that it intended to run the episode at a later date, though it was not scheduled by the time this book went to press.

Hodgins: This guy's wearing loafers. Aliens don't wear loafers.

Cam: Even if they want to pass unnoticed amongst us?

Booth: Before taking over?

Hodgins: This is harassment. You know, it's illegal to mock people for their fundamental beliefs.

On a lighter note, 'Spaceman in a Crater' is another example of the creative – and rather descriptive – titles the writers come up with for their episodes. Every title of a *Bones* episode refers in some way to the victim and the state in which the body was found. From 'The Man in the SUV' to 'Stargazer in a Puddle' the titles may seem reminiscent of *The Hardy Boys' Mysteries*, that had titles like *The House on the Cliff* or *The Secret of the Old Mill*. Executive producers Hart Hanson and Stephen Nathan admit that the titles serve a different, less romanticized purpose as well. Hanson explains that the rather literal title choices help keep the nearly two-dozen episodes per season straight in his mind. "Stephen has a huge, huge brain as you can see from his giant head," he jokes. "But, 'The Bodies in the Book'? I understand that. That's the one that had the bodies... in the book."

"'The Glowing Bones in the Old Stone House'?" Nathan cuts in. "That's the one with the old stone house where the body's bones glow... It's a little *Hardy Boys*, but it's mostly a remedial tool for us two guys who are still trying to figure out where to have lunch."

Radiolucence: Referring to the relative transparency in the passage of X-rays through a material. Radiolucent indicates a greater transparency, while radiodense indicates a greater level of opacity.

'Shipwrecked' by Shane Alexander
'Hold On To You' by Marjorie Fair, *Self Help Serenade*

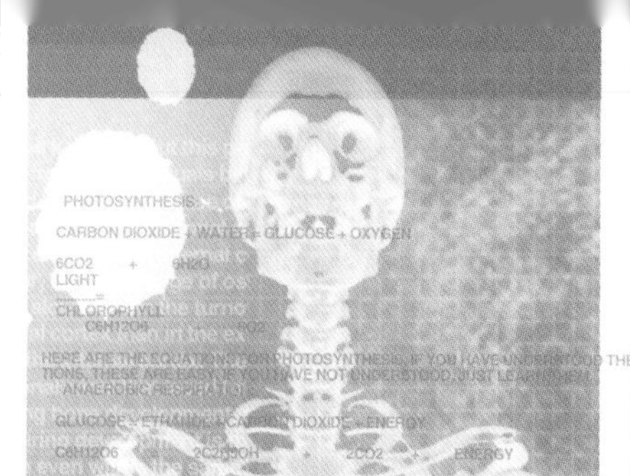

THE GLOWING BONES IN THE OLD STONE HOUSE

WRITTEN BY STEPHEN NATHAN *DIRECTED BY* CALEB DESCHANEL

GUEST STARRING: AJ BUCKLEY (DAN JANOV), BRIAN HALLISAY (BEN MICHAELSON), HILLARY TUCK (ABBY SINGER), DAN MARTIN (LT. JERRY FORBES), LARRY BATES (ERNIE SUMMERS), ANNA ZIELINSKI (CARLY VICTOR)

- A woman's remains found in an old house are the cause of concern because the bones are glowing. The luminescence, however, is not due to radiation, but rather **P. Phosphoreum** that had entered her bloodstream from a cut to her hand.
- Dr. Saroyan removes a desiccated finger and rehydrates it with a mixture of salt and fabric softener to obtain a fingerprint. The print is matched to celebrity chef Carly Victor.
- The body has multiple stab wounds. Incised cuts on the left radius and ulna are congruous with defensive injuries.
- The victim's friend, Abby, is found locked in the trunk of her car. There are blood traces on the dashboard and enough blood on the seat and the floor mat to prove that Carly was killed in the car. Semen and vaginal contributions in the backseat match Abby's husband, Ben, and Carly. A hairline fracture in Carly's skull was the result of her head hitting the dashboard, while trauma to the neck is determined to be whiplash.
- White shards found at the scene are from a ceramic knife that was shattered after it was used to kill Carly.
- Abby's bruising matches what she would have incurred if she was wearing a seatbelt while driving the car and slamming on the brakes. It is believed that this action forced Carly's head into the dashboard to disorient her, before Abby killed her for having an affair with Ben.

The latest case takes on a more personal aspect when Brennan realizes the victim is an acquaintance, a celebrity chef who was teaching her how to cook. This link helps the investigation, and helps Booth, who had been trying to get a reservation at the restaurant. Also helpful is the victim's MySpace page and links to other pages, where they find valuable clues and possible suspects. Once the case is solved, Brennan invites Booth over to make the late chef's famous recipe for macaroni and cheese.

Meanwhile, Hodgins insists that everything between him and Angela is fine, in spite of her repeated refusals to marry him. Their situation has Booth and Brennan – and later Booth and Cam – discussing their own feelings about love and marriage. When Angela suggests that part of the reason she can't say yes is because she has Brennan's ultra-rational voice in her head, it leads to a deeper conversation between the pair about Brennan's relationship issues. Later, using glowing sushi to spell out the words, Hodgins tells Angela that he loves her even if they aren't married, which prompts a proposal out of her that he accepts.

The production created actual MySpace pages for the guest characters in the episode, giving the viewers at home clues that could lead to the solution of the crime. "This episode was very complicated because there was tons and tons of stuff that tied into the MySpace pages for the characters," explains first A.D. Kent Genzlinger, "So we were on the internet as well as in the show. We had a lot of props to take photos of to give to video playback to put on the MySpace pages."

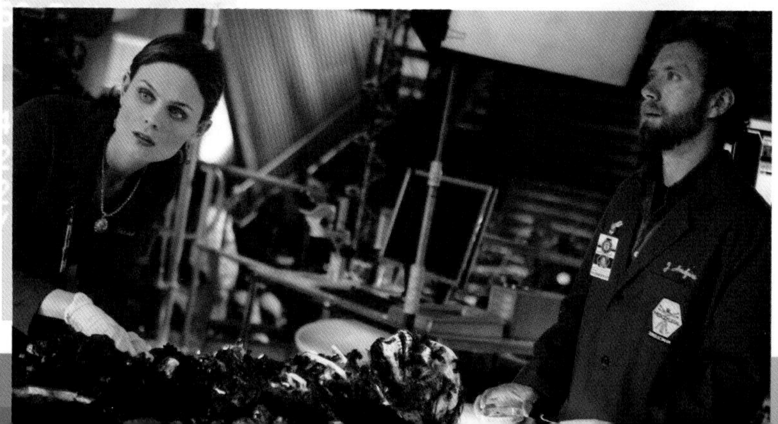

Booth: ...You believe in love, don't you?

Brennan: I believe that dopamine and norepinephrine stimulate euphoria because of certain biological triggers like scent, symmetrical features...

Booth: Symmetrical features?

Brennan: Yes. It's an indication of a good breeder. You appear to be a very good breeder.

Another complication came from the glowing bones in the title, as producer Jan DeWitt reveals, "*Bones* is a very quirky show. You never know what's going to come at you. You have a cabin way out in the woods where we find a glowing body. Well, how does the body glow? Should we put the glow inside the bone or should we paint it on and use a black light or should we just electrify it somehow? It took about a week for us to figure all that out. We did paint it on and use black lights. And it looked great."

A further unusual element of this episode was that it was directed by noted cinematographer and director Caleb Deschanel – Emily Deschanel's father. "It was hard to separate sometimes from the fact that he is my father," Emily Deschanel admits. "He'd tell me to sit up straight and stuff. The first day was really hard and then we kind of forgot about him being my dad and my being his daughter, for the most part. I'm hard on a lot of directors, but I was probably harder on him. And he was hard on us. He's tough, but he demands the best from everybody, which I think is such a good quality to have and it raises everything to another level."

P. Phosphoreum: Photobacterium Phosphoreum is a luminescent bacterium that lives in seafood. It emits a glow due to a chemical reaction with a catalyst known as luciferase.

'Cannonball' by Damien Rice, *O*
'Going Home' by MoZella, *I Will*
'Limbomaniacs' by Zeb, *Jesterized*
'Love is in the Air' by The Juan Maclean, *Less Than Human*

STARGAZER IN A PUDDLE

WRITTEN BY HART HANSON DIRECTED BY TONY WHARMBY

GUEST STARRING: RYAN O'NEAL (MAX KEENAN), PATRICIA BELCHER (ASST. U.S. ATTORNEY CAROLINE JULIAN), ROXANNE HART (CYNTHIA COLE), JOE NIEVES (JOE MELLON), CLEO KING (MINISTER SHEILA), ERIC STONESTREET (D.C. COP), LARISA MILLER (RUTH KEENAN), TRAVIS BRORSEN (STATE DEPARTMENT EMPLOYEE), BILLY F. GIBBONS (ANGELA'S DAD)

While working their latest case, Brennan is surprised by a visit from her father, who Booth is forced to arrest on the spot. The arrest is complicated when Booth must find a way to prove that Max Keenan is indeed Max Keenan in order to charge him. This gives father and daughter the time to reconnect, so Max can give Brennan a videotape of her mother. He also passes on an heirloom that will link her to her surviving family members, of whom she had no prior knowledge. Once Booth is able to prove Max's identity, he gets him to realize that he needs to turn himself in so that he doesn't abandon his daughter once again.

Angela and Hodgins are going full swing on their sudden wedding preparations. Angela asks Brennan to be her maid of honor, while Jack asks Zack to be his best man. Angela gets a yes, but Hodgins is told no. The President has requested that Zack go to Iraq in an official capacity. Zack worries that if something bad should befall him, he doesn't want his death to be tied to Jack's wedding memories. This forces Hodgins to ask Booth instead.

The wedding goes ahead as planned, until a representative from the State Department puts a stop to things by claiming that Angela is already married. Four years earlier she took part in a native marriage ceremony in Fiji that was legally binding. With a church full of guests, Hodgins and Angela flee to parts unknown, leaving Booth and Brennan standing at the altar with the minister.

The final episode of the second season brings some closure to the story of Brennan's parents, while opening up new areas to explore with relatives she's never known. The seriousness of this issue – along with the truly tragic case they're working on – is countered by the lightheartedness of Angela and Hodgins' wedding. It is, once again, that balancing act of comedy and drama that makes *Bones* so unique.

Brennan: I would like to marry you.

Booth: Kind of sudden, Bones. Let me think about that.

- The skeleton of what appears to be a child is found in the flooded foundation of a building.
- In spite of the tissue markers that Zack placed on the skull for a child, Angela's facial reconstruction matches that of an old woman. Degeneration in the collarbone and spiking on the superior articular process — combined with the fact that all the large bones in her body show osteolytis and advanced deterioration — implies that she was elderly. Brennan concludes that the victim suffered from a form of **progeria**.
- The sketch gets a hit off the NCIC database as a match for Chelsea Cole, aged twenty-two, who was diagnosed with a form of progeria that also left her with the mental age of a child.
- Upon seeing the medication being taken by the mother of the victim, Brennan concludes that the woman is suffering from HIV/AIDS.
- In the mud, along with the body, Hodgins finds a high concentration of dead **anostraca**. After conducting an experiment to determine if the anostraca could have died by feeding off poisoned flesh, they find that the victim was, in fact, poisoned by navirapine; an AIDS medication that links the murder to the mother.
- Brennan realizes that the mother's health had been deteriorating and she killed her daughter so that Chelsea would not be left unable to care for herself.

Co-executive producer (and the episode's director) Tony Wharmby fully appreciates the scripts from series creator Hart Hanson as they allow him to bring those elements out in his direction. "Hart always writes the scripts with the most subtext," says Warmby. "Although he smiles and denies it, and he's very self-deprecating in a charming way, from 'The Titan on the Tracks' all the way to this last episode, he's wonderful on subtext. You can dig deep into Hart's dialogue to find things rumbling under the surface. He manages to mix comedy, sadness and pathos, often all in the same scene. Some of the scenes in the last episode are quite hilarious, but also twist into something that has pathos and sadness and tragedy in it.

"There's a wonderful plot of this little girl who has disappeared and was probably murdered. In itself the situation and the circumstances of the story are extremely sad, and he manages to pull it off against the lightheartedness of the wedding; who's going to be best man, who's going to be the maid of honor and stuff like that. That's the skill of Hart's writing. I can study it and what I call 'mine the subtext', and that's for me – as a director and as a producer – like having a piece of gold in your hands."

Progeria: An aging disease that prevents the sufferer from entering puberty, but simultaneously ages his/her body.

Anostraca: Also known as fairy shrimp, these branchiopods are a group of primitive crustaceans that live in either fresh or saltwater.

'La Grange' by ZZ Top, *Tres Hombres*

'Blue Jean Blues' by ZZ Top, *Fandango*

'Gimme All Your Loving' by ZZ Top, *Eliminator*

SPECIAL AGENT SEELEY BOOTH

When a phone call came from the studio suggesting David Boreanaz might be interested in the role of Special Agent Seeley Booth, the actor was fresh off the success of *Buffy The Vampire Slayer* and *Angel*, where he played an extremely popular character for seven years in both series. Boreanaz was ready for something new. Creator/executive producer Hart Hanson remembers that in their initial meeting with Boreanaz, they struggled to convince him that Seeley Booth represented the departure he was looking for. "It wasn't a great meeting," Hanson admits. "However, a subsequent phone call assured him we weren't going to make him play Angel again."

As he learned more about what the part entailed, Boreanaz was able to pinpoint the many differences from the work he had done in the past. "I liked his complexity and his drive," Boreanaz explains. "I liked the fact that he was very open and sarcastic, and how he was in a relationship with someone like Bones; the way he really pushes her buttons constantly, and brings out the best in her and she brings out the best in him. I found him to be a really great character that I thought we could develop. You could see the character jump out at you from the page and there was room to grow with him and develop him. That's really what took me in for the role and also for seeing it as a series."

Seeley Booth was a character working through a dark, yet noble past. He grew up a street-smart kid from a humble background and served his country. There are definitely skeletons in his closet and the audience still does not know his entire history. Boreanaz provides a quick breakdown of the back-story: "He was in the service as a sniper and he was captured. While in captivity he was hit with bamboo sticks on his shins. He went through a pretty horrific time in the army and as a sniper who would take certain people out. That's just his life and his past story that we developed. The idea was brought to the table

"BEING A SNIPER, I TOOK A LOT OF LIVES. WHAT I'D LIKE TO DO BEFORE I'M DONE IS TRY AND CATCH AT LEAST THAT MANY MURDERERS."

According to prop master Ian Scheibel, most times David Boreanaz walks in front of the camera he is wearing or carrying the following items:

- A watch (Vintage Witnauer or an Omega Seamaster)
- Craps dice (from Hooters, Las Vegas)
- A "floaty" pen (the kind that makes the girl's clothes come off when you turn it upside down)
- His FBI ID
- A holstered sidearm (Glock)
- A Zippo Lighter
- $100 Poker Chip
- 3 by 5 index cards for field notes
- A Saint Christopher medal and chain

and we expanded on it from there."

Another important element of Booth's life that the audience did not learn about until the ninth episode of the first season is that he is the father of a young boy, Parker. The fact that he chose not to reveal such an important part of his life to Brennan and the squints until after they had built up his trust, provided much insight into his character.

Making Booth a dad obviously added an interesting layer to the character that Boreanaz could relate to. "Being a dad myself and having that kind of connection, I use that in my work a lot," he reveals. Never did that come more to bear than in the second season episode 'The Man in the Cell' in which Booth's child was potentially in mortal jeopardy. The episode required the actor to tap into some dark emotions. "It was terrifying," he admits, recalling how he felt thinking himself into that situation. "But it's part of the process of getting to the truth of the character and how he would feel under those horrifying circumstances."

Having a child also opened up questions about Booth's past relationships, namely with Parker's mother. We learn that he was never married, although he asked his girlfriend, Rebecca, to marry him as they waited for the result of her pregnancy test.

Booth continued a sexual relationship with Rebecca during the first two seasons, though his heart was saved for another.

All is not dark in Seeley Booth's world. Though his work as an FBI special agent certainly is, one of the highlights of his career is the relationship he's forged with Dr. Temperance Brennan, or, as he calls her, Bones. The playful banter and arguments these two characters share are the cornerstone of their relationship, but the tension here is not just sexual. "It's more intense actually than the sexual tension," writer/executive producer Stephen Nathan notes. Hart Hanson readily agrees: "Because the actors are both young, great-looking humans, you can't help but – it throws sex at you. At its heart though, I think we have a romantic comedy."

Booth and Brennan are quick to knock each other down, but even quicker at building one another up. They have a complex relationship, being partners, which would confuse any romantic relationship they might attempt. While it's clear that they have deep feelings for one another, they don't act on them for a variety of reasons, many of which seem to be little more than excuses.

Opposites most certainly attract when looking at Booth and Brennan. He's the more emotional, spiritual one, who is quick to jump to conclusions based on instinct,

but slower to act unless someone is in jeopardy or a killer may escape. He often has to rein Brennan in when she pays no heed to danger or red tape. But he also relies on her to back him up when needed.

Booth is the one who calls the scientists "squints", which is at first meant pejoratively, but is later embraced as a term of endearment. Though both Booth and Boreanaz are quick to note that Booth has no real relationship with the squints, when you watch the show that seems to be far from the truth. For example, Hodgins has become more of a sparring partner over the seasons and a begrudging friendship has developed; Angela and he share a playful flirtation, that neither intend to follow through on, but she is the first one he turns to when he needs a sympathetic ear or help with the emotional side of a case. Booth seems the least comfortable around Zack, but he's quick to step up and treat the awkward scientist with signs of respect, no matter how skewed they may be.

With the second season and the introduction of Camille Saroyan the audience gets another glimpse into Booth's character as he embarks on another largely sexual relationship with Cam.

"Cam is obviously someone in my past that I had a relationship with," Boreanaz notes, speaking for his character. "It was just kind of a fun, mostly sexual relationship. But we have respect for each other. We both understand the grittiness of the job. We could bond over that, where Booth couldn't bond over that with Bones."

That grittiness takes a darker turn in the second season when Booth is involved in the death of serial killer Howard Epps. The man literally slips through Booth's fingers – though Booth cannot be sure if Epps did actually slip or if he allowed him to fall. The degree to which that uncertainty affects Booth is a testament to the honor of his character. He may end the second season unclear about his future – and particularly his future with Brennan – but, like he does when dealing with his gambling addiction, Booth is going to continue to take things one day at a time.

DR. TEMPERANCE BRENNAN

Take one part Dr. Kathy Reichs, add a dash of her literary character, Temperance Brennan, mix thoroughly with the mind of Hart Hanson, and throw in a whole lot of Emily Deschanel and you get the television version of the title character. *Bones* is an ensemble show with a pair of leads, although there is no doubt that Dr. Temperance Brennan, as played by Emily Deschanel, is very much the core of the series. But with all those different ingredients making up the character, how did the actress first approach the role?

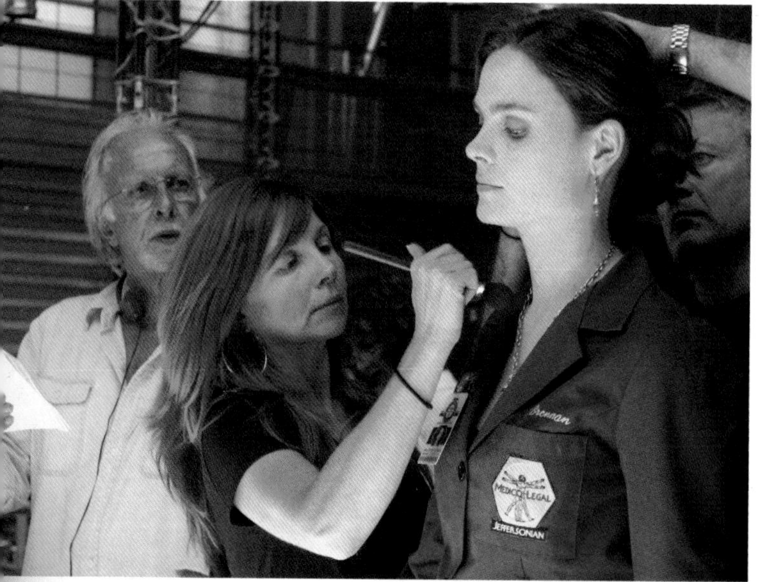

According to Deschanel, she started, logically enough, with what she was given. "I talked to Hart and he told me to take it from the script. I didn't want to read the books because they told me at the time that my character was not based on the Temperance in the books, so I didn't want that to influence me. I've read some since and there are similarities, but there are also definite differences. I didn't want to let certain things inform my depiction of the character that weren't intended to be a part of the television show. I took it at face value from the script and from my conversations with Hart and Barry and the director of the pilot, Greg Yaitanes. I just went from there."

Since that time, Deschanel has not only read some of the books but also met and discussed the character with Kathy Reichs herself, so she has been able to use that knowledge to inform her portrayal as well.

Deschanel was attracted to the character by her rich and unusual personality and back-story. "One of the biggest things that drew me to the character was playing a strong, intelligent woman who is independent and yet has things she needs to work on," she reveals. "She has a crazy past. Her personal life is kind of in disarray. A lot of times the characters that are offered to women have their personal lives figured out, but they don't really have a professional life. They're moms or they're wives or the girlfriend, those kinds

"MY MOST MEANINGFUL RELATIONSHIPS ARE WITH DEAD PEOPLE."

It seems odd to focus on the style of a character that hardly pays any attention to her style. But, in television, it takes a team of professionals to make the character look so stylishly unconcerned. The heads of the hair, makeup and costume departments explain how they create Brennan's distinctive look:

• Hair department head Bernie Gough: "Emily's character doesn't really pay that much attention to her hair, but obviously, for the screen, we do have to maintain it and keep it the same. Emily's really good; she's very flexible. As long as she okays it, she doesn't really want to think about it. She's usually more preoccupied with the science of it all than with her hair."

• Makeup department head Phyllis Temple: "They wanted to keep Brennan as natural as possible and not at all glamorous. Emily's very, very beautiful, so you have to be careful not to use too much. I just want to bring out her best features: she's got incredible eyes, so I just play her eyes up and try to keep everything else really natural."

• Costume designer Bobbie Read: "Because she's studied and traveled all over the world, I wanted to incorporate into her look things that she's picked up along the way, as well as keeping her natural looking, interesting and professional. It looks crisp, but it isn't. All the fabrics we put on her are natural because Emily's vegan. That means no wools, silks or leathers. That's always a bit challenging with the shoes, but we've got it down now. I've tried to make her look professional, but still have a softer side.

of archetypes, but they don't have the business aspect of their lives figured out. In Temperance you have a character that really has her stuff together when it comes to her job and her area of expertise – she's passionate about it and she's really good at it. But her personal life needs a little help, though she's been growing throughout the two seasons that we've had."

When the audience first meets Brennan in the pilot she throws a Homeland Security Agent to the ground and starts issuing orders to his men – and they follow her. She is at once seen as being both tough and smart. But, at the same time, those traits offset the awkward way she navigates through the real world, unable to connect with average people or enjoy simple pleasures without analyzing them. "She's not used to being open to her feelings," explains Deschanel. "She's learned how to suppress everything; however, through knowing Booth and Angela, she's discovering how to open up to her different feelings. And it's scary, figuring out different things about her past and who she is and who her family is, and what that means for her and her life; all that is kind of overwhelming."

What Brennan lacks in her own emotional life, she makes up for with her friendships. Choosing the perceptive artist, Angela, as a best friend shows that Brennan is at least seeking out the traits that would balance her out. The same can be said of her partnership with Booth. Though much of the focus of the show is on the differences between Brennan and Booth, it follows the basic structure of romantic comedy that opposites do attract.

Though, having said that, it's important to note that their relationship goes much deeper than the simple romantic comedy formula. Many of Brennan's personal difficulties seem to stem from her childhood. "I think she is so used to people abandoning her," Deschanel notes. "Her parents left when she was fifteen and, although she's starting to understand why that happened and that they were perhaps doing it for her own good, she still feels abandoned. Her brother Russ left when, in her mind, he didn't even have to. And it turns out her father is this bad guy; he kills people. She doesn't really trust men, and I think she expects everyone to leave. But

here is Booth who sticks through it all; he is there through the worst of it – her discoveries about her father and her family. He's really there to talk to her and comfort her, but not in a sappy way, in a very tough, comforting way. And that's exactly what she needs. She doesn't need somebody to be soft with her."

Not that the life of this forensic anthropologist and author is all drama and upset. Granted, her idea of a vacation is helping identify bodies in a mass grave, but she does know how to kick back and have fun. She is also able to explore sexual relationships, like her male counterpart, Booth, no matter that they often end badly.

She enjoys a wonderful camaraderie with her co-workers and has more than earned their esteem. In the first season, Dr. Goodman was in awe of her abilities, yet also took her under his wing and attempted to help her with her emotional development. Her doctoral student, Zack, looks up to her and even developed a bit of a crush on her that has evolved into a more friendly relationship. Even Hodgins, who has the power behind his name to throw his weight around, defers to his boss and wants nothing more than her utmost respect.

Still, all the positive experiences in her life are balanced against her traumatic past and the challenges it continues to present. "At the end of the last season she finds out her name isn't even Temperance; it's Joy," Deschanel continues. "Which is crazy. She was intended to be Joy – to have joy. She has joy and she's had so much more joy in her life from knowing Booth and Angela and all the squints, but she's a lonely person too. I think that everyone can relate to that on certain levels: everyone feels alone at different times. Even as the world gets more and more overpopulated, everyone understands that feeling of being alone." As the second season ends with Booth at her side, it seems unlikely that she will be alone forever.

ANGELA MONTENEGRO

Angela Montenegro is the Jeffersonian's resident forensic artist, with an emphasis on the *artist* portion of that title. She's an expert in facial reconstruction, which entails much more than simply putting pencil to paper or inputting information in the holographic imager. To properly sketch a person from a set of remains requires some insight into character, something that Angela excels at. Michaela Conlin recalls that this was an intrinsic aspect of the character right from the start. "The original character description said she had a minor in psychology," she reveals, "which is really interesting. I think that she has a really intuitive nature, a very emotional aspect." That emotional aspect not only serves the character in her work, but in her friendship with Brennan and her relationship with Hodgins as well.

"She's an artist in a world of scientists," Conlin continues. "I think that's really nice to have as part of the show. Angela brings this alternative perspective: she doesn't see them as bones, rather she sees the life and the body – the victim behind the bones. She's many things – she's definitely a nerd at heart. She really relates to these people who want to find the truth, which is what she's really all about; she's a very honest person. I think on some level that it makes sense to her that they're always trying to figure out what really happened. She also has just grown to love the job and the opportunity."

Angela's job has expanded as the series has grown. Considering that the character says early in the first season that it's the longest she has ever held any job, it would seem that, as uncomfortable as it can be at times, she has found her niche. Booth often uses her to connect with the families of victims, or even with suspects. In the season two episode 'The Man in the Cell' Hodgins refers to her in a newspaper article as being the 'heart' of the squints. And that is certainly true of her relationship with her boss and best friend, Brennan. Angela is the first person everyone seeks out for advice on matters of love and life.

The fact that Angela has so many interesting facets to her personality is something that attracted Conlin to the role right from her first encounter with the character. "I

"I'M NOT DRIVEN BY THE NEED FOR JUSTICE AND ALL THAT. I'M A GOOD TIME GIRL."

remember saying to my agent, 'This guy understands how to write for women'," she says, recalling her first impression of Hart Hanson. "It's really hard to find that in episodic television. I remember very much responding to that."

However, just because Conlin responded to the role, there was no guarantee that the production would respond to her. "I don't think people realize what you have to do to get a job in network television," notes Conlin of the grueling audition process. "A lot of people have to say yes to you. There are the producers and the studio and the network, as well as the chemistry reads and the table reads to go through. It's pretty crazy, but it's fun too," she says with a smile. Conlin's training as an actress helped her cope with the demanding auditions. "There's something that I really love about testing, because it's very theatrical," she explains. "I've studied theatre for a long time, so it's nice. You kind of get in this arena where it's like, who's going to be left standing? For me, personally, I just really enjoy that. Barry and Hart were so supportive of me throughout the process. For me, it was very easy. I don't know if everyone can say that but, for me, it was fun."

One of the most interesting aspects of Angela's character is that, as fun and freewheeling as she may be, she's clearly been hurt in the past. Over the course of the series, she has made numerous seemingly lighthearted comments that imply some deeper issues with the opposite sex. Even Brennan wonders aloud at one point what kind of men Angela has dated to inspire those comments. The season one episode

'The Skull in the Desert' was a powerful showcase of how closed off she can be. During the episode it is revealed that she is the one responsible for keeping a man that she loved at arm's length.

These hints at a darker past make her relationship with Hodgins all the more important. What started out as merely a workplace flirtation slowly built into something more. Interestingly enough, the emotional Angela was the one who fought it every step of the way. "She's grown a lot," Conlin says of her character's emotional journey on the show. "She's involved in a really serious relationship now, which I don't think she ever in a million years would have imagined possible, especially in the pilot. I feel like she's definitely become a little bit more stable. I think she's still kind of crazy and out there, but her feet are on the ground when she's at work."

Part of Angela's craziness is reflected in her wardrobe. Though always business appropriate, she has a flamboyant style that Conlin credits to the show's costume designer. "It's all Bobbie Read," she says. "She is wonderful. I love her. I think she's great. She has been with us from the pilot and gives us a lot of freedom to say 'I like this. I don't like this.' She really knows what's going to work on us. We just shot the proposal scene and we fitted a few different dresses. She really wanted me to wear this one dress, and I said no – but she's always right."

"Angela is my favorite to dress," admits Bobbie Read, "because she's an interesting bohemian character. I'm always trying to push the envelope with her. Michaela is more conservative in real life, but we have great fun dressing her." That sense of fun even translates to her Jeffersonian uniform. "Angela decorated her lab coat," Read continues. "Being the creative art type, we decorated her coat as though she had done it herself. We'll do another one next year."

Whether it's in her outfits, her work as an artist, or the sarcastic comments she bandies about, Angela is not afraid to express herself. Of course, no one would expect anything less from the daughter of a man who looks very much like a member of ZZ Top.

DR. ZACK ADDY

He started out as a Dr. Brennan's doctoral student, following in her footsteps and developing a little crush on her in the process. Zack Addy served an essential role in the creation of the series, as more than just the adorably clueless man-child. "If we were on cable TV, it's possible we would have given Brennan Asperger's Syndrome," reveals Hart Hanson. "Somebody who is extremely detached from their feelings and very, very rational, who rationalizes everything. On a network show you don't want your leads lumbered with something like that, so you give it to someone else. Zack is the ideal hyper-rationalist. You know that underneath Brennan's empirical, rational surface is a passionate woman. With Zack, we've always said, he is slightly alien. He watches people to see what the humans do; he's learning human behaviors. It's like he's from another planet and he's studying us."

Hanson recalls that Eric Millegan was one of the first actors cast in the series. For Millegan, the ease of his casting was something new and wonderful, having spent years in New York auditioning for stage plays. "The casting director brought me in to audition for our producers, Hart Hanson and Barry Josephson, and the director Greg Yaitanes," he recalls. "I did the scene for them and they seemed to really like it and I thought, 'This is going well.' So it was very simple – four auditions and I had the part. I mean there's so much competition but, once you get to that studio test, you're one of four or five people. At that stage it's like, 'Oh my God, I can taste it!' In three weeks I had a television pilot. It was the most exciting time of my life and my career. I had auditioned for years in New York and most of the time I wasn't working. I was on Broadway for five months over a ten-year span. I feel very blessed to have gotten the show."

One of the earliest relationships established on the series was that between Zack and Brennan. He served to humanize the title character through the way that she protected him, and also he proved that she was not alone in her oddly scientific and incredibly intelligent ways. "She's Zack's mentor and there was a little bit of a crush," explains Millegan. "I say 'was' because we haven't really touched on that for a while. Certainly Emily and I became friends immediately. The off-camera relationship is that she has become one of my best friends. It's very supportive." Millegan was new to Los Angeles when *Bones* began filming, and he is quick to cite the immediate friendships he struck up with his fellow castmembers as being one of the things he loves about the show.

"WE'RE CRIME FIGHTERS."

Though he is one of the oldest of the actors on the show, Millegan's more boyish qualities serve his character well. What could come across as off-putting behavior from the ultra-intelligent character is far more endearing because of the naïveté that Millegan brings to the role. The rest of the characters may shake their heads in despair at times, but they also want to protect Zack, which is why they put up with his eccentricities.

Those boyish traits have made it necessary for Zack to do some growing up along the way. "This year, my character – after working on it for a long time – was finally awarded his doctorate in the middle of the season, and we settled on a haircut that now we're sticking with," Millegan confirms, with a some relief in his voice. "I was kind of like lonely, adorable Zack last season and they've really pushed me to grow up, come into my own, and become a man on the show; so that's been exciting. Though even now they're still saying to Zack, 'Be more authoritative. You know what you're talking about now. Be a professional.' It's exciting that my character is really changing as the show goes on."

Alongside Hodgins, Zack is responsible for some of the lighter moments in the series. TJ Thyne calls them the Bert and Ernie of the show, referring to the equally awkward best friends from *Sesame Street*. With their 'King of the Lab' contest, their weirdly exuberant experiments, and Friday-night beetle races, Zack and Hodgins are a team unlike any other on television. "I think my favorite scene ever was with TJ and I in the Vegas episode [season two's 'The Woman in the Sand'] where I punched him," Millegan notes. "That was really fun, and it was probably the longest and the most dialogue I've ever had in a scene. It was real; it was almost a theatrical scene. Because it was the two of us, it was some really fun acting, and TJ was great. That's a scene that I remember very well. It wasn't in the script, initially. They were a little short on time, so they said, 'Let's toss in a TJ and Eric scene.' And that was great. It kind of worked almost as a little play unto itself."

The one character on the show that, on the surface, seems unwilling to get close to Zack is Booth. But saying that, there have been moments where Booth has looked past the odd scientist and placed an open hand on his shoulder, which is often seen as a sign of approval among males. "He definitely cares about me, but he has his distance." Millegan says of the Booth/Zack relationship, speaking as his character. "He saved me in the explosion scene [in the second season episode 'The Man in the Cell']. He was right there. Not that he – why would he let me die? But our relationship grows a little bit at the end of the second season because I ask him questions about what it's like to go to war. As he has experience in the military as an army Ranger and sniper, I ask him what it's like to be shot at. There was a little bit of real male bonding there for a second, right at the end of the episode, that I'm glad to have had."

Millegan is referring to a scene in which he is preparing to go off to Iraq, in an unexpected move for the character that comes at the end of the second season. "I think that grows him up as well," Millegan says of Zack's surprise adventure abroad. "He has a whole new experience and we'll find out what happens to him there." Certainly, whatever does happen it will be interesting to watch as the repercussions play out over season three.

DR. JACK HODGINS

He is the sole heir to the Cantilever Group, the third largest privately owned corporation in the country. He is a conspiracy theorist who weaves wild tales of government cover-ups. He is one half of the adorably cute couple known as 'Hodgela'.

And yes, he is the bug man.

"That is the part of the character where there is no parallel with TJ," says the actor himself – TJ Thyne – focusing on the "bug man" description of his character. "Oh man, if I'm sitting there and start feeling something with a lot of legs crawling on me somewhere... Bleck! I hate it," he continues, laughing at his own squeamishness. "Jack would probably reach down, pick it up, and identify its origin, stage of growth and three names for it, all in thick Latin, before setting it free. Bugs and slimy things, nope, not a TJ thing at all. I hope you can't tell though or I'm not doing my job as an actor!"

Though Hodgins takes pride in being the bug man, that is only one of the many components of his persona. "Jack has a lot of personalities we still haven't even seen yet," reveals Thyne. "I *love* that! The fact that the audience has yet to see every color in Jack's palette. There is a lot of who Jack is that we still don't know and that we'll get to see in season three." Thyne's excitement over the future of his character is nothing compared to the joy he's experienced playing Jack Hodgins so far.

"Up until now, this much we do know," Thyne says, providing a run down of exactly who his character is. "Dr. Jack Hodgins works at the Jeffersonian Institute, along with Dr. Brennan and under Cam, as an expert scientist with three advanced degrees in entomology, botany, and mineralogy. He's smart, really smart, and not just book smart: Jack's got a whole lot of street smarts in him. He's also obscenely rich and is the largest donor to the Jeffersonian Institute, which ultimately makes Jack everyone's boss!

"Jack has an enormous heart," Thyne continues, with obvious affection for his onscreen counterpart. "He hides it from most people and on most days, but he's passionate as hell. He is madly in love with Angela. Really. Mad love. He adores the team he gets to work with, though again, it's not in his nature to say it out loud, unless it's to Angela."

"I AM THE BUG MAN."

Hodgins provides a lot of the comic relief in this romantic comedy. It could be the role that TJ Thyne was born to play as his natural enthusiasm is incredibly infectious and contributes to a character who – on paper – could otherwise come across as rather annoying. Think about it. A wealthy conspiracy theorist, who is also a nerd and a brainiac, is not someone most people would be rushing to be friends with. Yet, the way the character is written, combined with the charming way that Thyne portrays him, has made Jack Hodgins a fan favorite.

The meeting of actor and character seemed perfect from the start. "The casting process was pretty excellent," Thyne recalls. "I got a chance at my first audition to meet Hart Hanson, the creator of *Bones* and thus the creator of all of our characters; so, I guess that makes him our God. Ha, the God of *Bones*! I should call him that... Okay, maybe not," he says with a laugh. "Hart is amazing. He's smart, so smart, very witty, blunt, kind and serious about his work. It has been said a lot recently that the character of Jack is the onscreen representation of Hart, and I have to agree with that. Hart Hanson – his name is the very description of what he ultimately is: all heart."

In fact Thyne seems most at ease when discussing matters of the heart. "I'm much more about the relationships Jack has than about his bugs and slime," he admits. "I identify with the passion he feels for Angela; the older-brother mentality he has with Zack; his budding friendship with Cam; and his ongoing, always growing, relationships with Brennan and Booth.

"He's simple at heart," Thyne continues. "He loves Angela, and what she loves is what matters to him. Taking her to the swings because that's what she always remembers as a kid [on their first date in the second season episode 'The Girl with the Curl'] is the way Jack thinks. I love that

about him. I think that is a really important quality to have in real life. And guys, this is a note for all of us, it's so important to listen to the women in our lives, and really hear them and what they ultimately and truly want – not what we think they might want. It is the only way to be. I really loved asking Angela to marry me... three times! And the wedding! And Jack coming to the discovery that he loves this woman no matter what, and however, whatever she wants, is great with him, so long as he gets to be with her."

How he got to be with her is an interesting lesson in the development of an on-going television series. "You spend a little time with actors, and you start seeing what they can do," explains creator/executive producer Hart Hanson, speaking about the Hodgins and Angela relationship. "And there they were, TJ Thyne and Michaela Conlin. There they were working together the way Booth and Brennan were and, again, they're both lovely looking, and you could see it starting to work. They're both very good actors. It's been really fun for us, while we're keeping one couple apart to put the other together."

The way Hodgins and Angela came together was unusual for a television series, too. Their relationship grew slowly with flirtation and hints of jealousy. And it progressed uniquely as well. "So far – I don't know if anyone's noticed – we're not putting them through hell," notes Hanson. "They're a pretty good couple. They may have their obstacles and their ups and downs and everything, but it's not like they're breaking up and getting back together all the time or anything like that. It has been a slow build towards a relationship." That build is important to the series as a whole because it serves a significant purpose. "It is a bit of an escape valve for the audience," offers writer/executive producer Stephen Nathan. "You just release a little bit of steam every now and then... And that relationship is just working out beautifully."

DR. DANIEL GOODMAN

Part administrator, part father figure, Dr. Daniel Goodman played many roles in *Bones* over the course of the first season. This was as much due to the actor's ability to grow with the character as it was the writers' attempts to determine exactly who that character could be. As mentioned earlier, the difficulty the writers had in servicing the character was that Goodman, by his very nature as an administrator, would often take the show out of the mystery. That's not to say that he did not serve a purpose and play an important part in establishing the series.

Goodman is as intelligent and as much of a scientist as the rest of the squints, but he is also the most well rounded and professional of the team. Aside from Angela, he would be the one you could most easily trot out at parties and fundraising events to dazzle the guests and help ease some contributions from their wallets. But it is his contributions to Brennan's character that proved most useful in the first season of the show.

Bones as a series is hung on the premise that Brennan wanted to be more involved in fieldwork. Yet, at the same time, this fiercely independent character did not like to be told where to go and what to do by her FBI handler. Since Booth had no real power over her, it often fell to Goodman to provide the impetus for Brennan to join Booth in a case or to travel across the country with him. This permitted some reluctance in the early stages of the Brennan and Booth relationship, though it was clear that both characters enjoyed being together. Goodman took these assignments a step further by suggesting Brennan use the opportunity to open herself up to new experiences.

A family man in his home life, Goodman often took a paternal role with the squints. He was the one who was finally able to put into words the important work Angela did when she experiences an emotional crisis with her job in the episode 'A Boy in a Bush'. Along with Hodgins, Goodman attempted to kick start Zack into growing up and finishing his doctoral thesis, moving past his crush on Brennan to take responsibility for his life. Even when butting heads with Hodgins during 'A Woman at the Airport', Goodman managed to be the better man, and they both learned something from the exchange. And it's hard to forget that Goodman was the first of the squints to whom Booth confided he had a son.

In spite of the important character developments Goodman played a hand in, by the end of the first season the writers were having more and more of a difficult time finding a role for the character within the individual episodes. The tough decision then fell to Hart Hanson to accept that they would have to release the actor that everyone had so enjoyed working with. "One thing that'll never happen on our show is that no one's ever going to find out they're off the show in a script," Hanson says, emphatically. "We don't lie. They're a great bunch of people; they deserve to know the truth. When we decided that Jonathan Adams was not going to work for us, I made the call myself. I think you owe that to actors."

"I'M AN ARCHEOLOGIST. MY FINDINGS WILL BE CONGRUENT WITH THE FACTS."

DR. CAMILLE SAROYAN

"We were going to kill her at episode six," creator/executive producer Hart Hanson recalls with a small amount of glee in his voice. "I think it was Stephen [Nathan] and I who started thinking we couldn't kill her. We said, 'We don't want to kill her at episode six now, we want to kill her in episode thirteen.' Meanwhile, we were hoping to show them [the fans and the studio] that she shouldn't die, and that's in fact what happened. It was always a possibility, but we just had a tremendous amount of faith in Tamara and Camille – what she was giving us and how that character could grow."

Dr. Camille Saroyan was brought in to allow the writers to open up the mysteries, and focus on the bodies as well as the bones. As the new head of forensics, she would naturally butt heads with Dr. Brennan, but they soon fell into a comfortable working relationship, once they learned how to deal with their vastly different approaches to the work.

The difficulty that Cam may have had coming into the new situation was nothing like what the actress, Tamara Taylor, experienced when she started working on the show: "I was really nervous," Taylor admits. "It was like the first day of school. It could have been really hard, but I felt immediately welcome. It was actually fun, terrifying and fun. It's a rare and beautiful moment when talent and kindness come in the same package. It often doesn't happen that way, so I feel grateful that it does with this show."

In describing Cam, Taylor cuts right to the chase. "Clearly, she's the boss. She's good at what she does. She's ambitious, but also fun-loving and easy-going. They've described her as – not one of the guys – but as someone who likes to throw back a shot and play some poker on her days off. So she's an interesting paradox. It's fun to walk the tightrope and try to make sense of that."

Cam had had a relationship with Booth in the past, which is briefly rekindled. Though it's often been described as a purely sexual relationship, Taylor doesn't see it that way. "Maybe I'm just a simpleton, but I don't know any woman that can disassociate in that way. I would like to think it is more than that for her. She's met her match in Booth. What will come of that, I don't know. It may be unrequited, but she's met her match."

Dr. Saroyan's businesslike focus is always on solving the crime over finding the truth. Early on, this approach often found her at odds with the team, but the dynamic grew and changed. "They're all really good at what they do," Taylor reflects. "They're oddballs, and consumed by their jobs in a way that she appreciates. They're funny – Zack and Hodgins together are hysterical. Their zeal about every single madcap idea they have – it's just so fun to watch the two of them play off each other. She also appreciates what Angela and Hodgins have. I think within Cam's hard shell there's the soft person who gets love and romance and wants it for herself; and so, I think, she is rooting for Angela and Hodgins." That hard shell is weakening as she continues to establish herself at the Jeffersonian and become a vital member of the close-knit squint team.

"EVERY CIRCUS NEEDS A RINGMASTER. IN THIS CIRCUS, IT'S ME."

GROSS ANATOMY

SPECIAL EFFECTS MAKEUP: CREATING THE DEAD BODIES

Without the bodies to examine, an episode of Bones would be... well, considerably shorter to say the least. The amazingly well crafted and often disturbing creations are the work of Chris and Kevin Yagher and their team of special effects makeup artists. Each piece is lovingly made with great attention paid to detail. Chris Yagher explains the process:

When creating a dead body for the show, we usually start by confirming with the producers the age and gender of the victim. This information will let us know which skeleton to use. Obviously, age will tell us about the victim's size in most cases, whereas the gender will let us know more about the shape of the skeletal structure. For instance, the pelvic girdle of a female is more rounded than that of a male.

We then determine if there are any markings on the bones. Are there bullet holes, knife marks or fractures? Did the victim have a bone disease? In one case, during season one ['The Woman at the Airport'], a female victim had skull alterations from cosmetic surgery. Once we make any necessary bone markings, we proceed by putting flesh on the bones.

The look of the skin and flesh will change depending upon the answers to a number of questions, such as: how long has the victim been dead? Was the body outside and exposed to weather conditions? Was there any animal and bug activity? How was the victim murdered? The answers to those questions will help us determine what materials to use for the flesh, how much flesh to put on the bones, the coloring and texture of the flesh and any particular markings that need to be made in the flesh.

We complete the look of the dead body by creating the bodily fluids and matter that may seep out from and surround the victim at the crime scene. These substances include blood, organ fluids, brain matter and other decomposing excretions.

Most of our research for the look of the bodies is done by looking at medical books and by gathering information on the internet. Initially, I was very surprised at the number of websites that contain rather explicit material involving the dead! Although public access to such material may be controversial, they have been a great source to us while creating victims for the show.

Donna Cline, the show's technical consultant, has also been very helpful to us in researching how the dead bodies should look. For the second season episode 'The Bodies in the Book' there are three victims that have been ravaged by three different creatures: crabs, rats and fire ants. Donna showed us pictures of dead bodies with bite marks from each of them. She has also given us helpful descriptions, such as: how bodies will burn depending upon the accelerant used, what parts of the body will be eaten first by animals and how the coloring of decomposing flesh and fluids change when exposed to different elements.

Besides dead bodies, we have created a number of make-up prosthetics. For instance, we created diseased skin and bullet hole prosthetics for the episode 'The Man in the SUV'. We also created a Y-incision chest appliance for an autopsy scene in 'The Boy in the Shroud'. For the episode 'Aliens in a Spaceship' we created an inflamed, bulbous-looking shin appliance for when Hodgins suffers from compartment syndrome. We have also created a number of special props, including a charred lung, a child's finger, eyeballs, an alien-like bone implant, tattooed skin flaps and even bear scat.

Clockwise from this picture: The first body from 'Bodies in the Book'; the third body from the same episode, bitten by fire ants; Caroline Epps' severed head from 'The Man in the Cell' was so realistic it almost made Hart Hanson sick!

GETTING UNDER THE SKIN
THE SCIENCE OF BONES

It all comes back to the science.

Bones is a series about mystery and romance. It's both a comedy and a drama. But one of the main things that sets it apart from many other shows on television is that it brings the unique science of forensic anthropology to the screen. And, though the science is never intended to be more than a backdrop for the mysteries and the characters, it is an essential part of the show. "It has to be real," insists creator/executive producer Hart Hanson, "which means, by the way, that we're probably sixty-five to seventy percent accurate. We condense things – you get DNA results in an afternoon, that kind of stuff; though you can get DNA results quickly. We don't put things in a machine and spit out the name of the person. There are some shows where there's a secret machine where you put in some blood and you get their address – which would be a good machine!"

The writers may take some dramatic license in the interests of storytelling, but they also strive to present the truth as much as they can. To help with that, Dr. Kathy Reichs is not only the inspiration for the show, she's also a producer. "My role is mainly to work with the writers and the researcher and help them get the science," Reichs reveals. "They'll have a story idea and they'll ask me questions, such as: 'How could you make this work? How could you make it look like somebody was squashed by a building? Or fell out of an airplane? What would you see in the bones?' Then, when the script is finished, I read it and give them suggestions, mainly with regard to the science."

In addition to Kathy Reichs' contributions, the production employs a full-time technical advisor on set to answer any and all questions that come up, and to serve as the storyboard artist, drawing up all of Angela's creations. Described as "the real life Angela", Donna Cline is the forensic artist responsible for making sure *Bones* is always focused on the bones. "My process has become more and more refined as we go along through the seasons, which is great," notes Cline. "What I do is, when I get the script, I analyze it for accuracy, for props, for visual content, for wardrobe – any kind of notes that I have that might interact with what they do. I also do what I call 'actor packets', for the episode. These are dialogue sides that I basically Xerox right out of medical dictionaries. I go through and provide the actors with the anatomical locations of everything that they have to talk about. If it's a proximal phalanges they know what it looks like and where it is. So they go into these scenes knowing where it is and how to say it."

Cline's value, however, is for more than just textbook definitions. Having spent years doing what it is that the squints on *Bones* do, she brings firsthand knowledge of the job to the production. "The other thing that I work with the cast on is body language," she continues. "Contextual understanding of how to approach a certain kind of scene. For example, if it's a crime scene or in a lab or a body somewhere, how would they approach that? What are they looking for? What is the second sense that's going on internally for their character? What are they scanning the environment for? So it's actually about the psychology and the experiential aspects of how you are around human remains."

As important as it is to get the science right, the writers don't spend a lot of time dwelling on it within the episode. They acknowledge it, they explain it, and then they move on from it without worrying too much about the audience keeping up with the minutiae. "I think the audience has come to trust that what we're saying is probably true," writer/executive producer Stephen Nathan says. "In the same way that when you watch *ER*, you don't really need to know what the medication they're giving that patient is really doing, just whether it seems accurate and sounds good. That's not why you're watching the show. On *CSI* that might be more why you're watching the show – to really find out those forensic clues. But we want to get to the humor."

Hart Hanson agrees it's important to keep the characters' priorities straight. He adds, smiling, "Yeah, they have to argue about God."